TEACHER'S GUIDE

Contents

Longman

Longman Group UK Limited
Longman House, Burnt Mill, Harlow,
Essex CM20 2JE, England
and Associated Companies throughout the world.

First published 1985
Third impression 1986

ISBN 0-582-51078-3

Set in Times New Roman 11/13
Printed in Great Britain by
Butler & Tanner Ltd, Frome and London

Acknowledgements

We are grateful to the following for permission to reproduce copyright poems:

J. Curwen & Sons Ltd for an adapted version of 'Here is a Beehive' by Emilie Poulson;
Longman Group Ltd for an adapted version of 'Abracadabra wizzy woo' from page 11 *Songs
and Rhymes For The Teaching of English* by Julian Dakin (1968); Penguin Books Ltd for an
adapted version of 'This is the father short and stout' from page 14 *This Little Puffin . . .
Nursery Songs and Rhymes* compiled by Elizabeth Matterson.

Introduction

1 Aims

Way in aims to give primary and early primary children an introduction to English.

Way in aims to give these learners a limited amount of useful language items.

Way in provides a basis for reading and writing.

Way in encourages a positive attitude towards learning English.

2 Main features

a *Way in* lays a foundation for the beginning stages of reading. *Way in* incorporates 'Look and Say' (whole word and sentence matching), the phonic reading approach and letter recognition.

b *Way in* provides a language load appropriate for the young beginner. A restricted amount of language has been deliberately chosen for *Way in*. It is simple and related to the child's needs and interests. When the children have mastered these language items they can proceed to a more structured and graded course for primary classes.

c *Way in* teaches the alphabet. The children learn to recognize the letters of the alphabet, both lower case and capitals. A systematic approach is provided by sensitizing the children to the letters and their sound values in *Way in A*. In *Way in B* they also learn the names of the letters.

d *Way in* teaches writing. The very young beginner needs to be taught how to form letters. In *Way in A* the children practise handwriting patterns and proceed to letter shapes. They then write the letters in words they know and can recognize. In *Way in B* they also practise writing short sentences.

e *Way in* ensures that English is fun to learn. Every lesson includes games and activities and each unit has a song or rhyme in it. The children are actively involved in learning English.

f *Way in* makes all other primary courses accessible to the children.

3 Content and characters

The content of *Way in* has been selected on the basis of two main factors: topic and language. The topics chosen focus on the children's interests. Between the ages of three and six they like to count, learn the names of the primary colours, and identify the things around them. In *Way in* these concepts are presented through full colour pictures illustrating a situation or short story.
There are five characters in *Way in*. They all live on the beach. The animal characters appear in *Way in A* and Pam, a little girl, is introduced in *Way in B*. They are:
Drago – a mischievous and scatterbrained dragon. He loves playing jokes on his friends.
Belinda – an elephant who enjoys lazing in the sun more than anything.
Otto – an octopus who uses all his tentacles for many different jobs.
Tubs – a turtle who is rather miserable at times.
Pam – a 6-year-old girl who lives near the beach.

4 Lesson scheme

Way in A contains sufficient material for 45 lessons as does *Way in B*, making a total of 90 lessons. In some school or learning situations one book will be used during one year and in others both books will be used in one year. Each lesson contains enough material for a thirty minute classroom period.

The course material is organized into units.
Way in A = 15 units.
Way in B = 15 units.

Each unit = 3 lessons.

Lesson 1 = 1st presentation page + activity.
Lesson 2 = 2nd presentation page + 1st workpage + song.
Lesson 3 = 2nd workpage + song.

5 Language

In *Way in* the language is simple and carefully controlled. In *Way in A* there are 58 vocabulary items and 7 sentence patterns. In *Way in B* there are 28 new vocabulary items and 7 new sentence patterns. (See language charts on pages 10–13.)

Way in prepares the children for many primary courses which they will eventually go on to. In particular it leads into *Pathway*, a six-stage course written by Donald Dallas and Nicolas Hawkes and published by Longman. Most of the vocabulary items and sentence patterns in *Way in* are found in *Pathway 1*. *Way in* therefore provides an excellent introduction to that primary course.

The alphabet

Both lower case and capital letters are presented in *Way in*. The former are taught in *Way in A* and the latter in *Way in B*. In order to sensitize the children to the alphabet in a meaningful way the letters are presented systematically throughout the course. In *Way in A* their sounds and their shapes are presented while the children are learning to understand and to speak the words which begin with those letters. For example, in *Way in A*, in Unit 2 'bird' and 'balloon' and 'kite' are taught. In that particular lesson the teacher concentrates on the shapes of 'b' and 'k' and their sounds. Thus the recognition of shapes, their sounds and the meaning of the word itself is integrated. From Unit 7 of *Way in A* onwards the children learn how to form the letters they have already learnt to recognize. These are now introduced in families of similarly formed letters. Hence 'c' and 'o' and 'a' are presented together, as are 'r' 'm' and 'n'. Grouping them in this way enables the children to form the letters more easily. Each new letter is immediately written in a word and an illustration of that word given so that the children can see the relationship of the letter to the word and its meaning. By the end of *Way in A* the child recognizes every lower case letter, and knows its sound and how to form it.

In *Way in B* capital letters are taught. On the activity pages of the first nine units the lower case and its capital appear side by side so the children can see the relationship between them. The capitals appear in alphabetical order, grouped in threes, i.e. in Unit 1 a A, b B, and c C are taught. This provides a reference point for the child. In these early units the child learns the shape of the capital letter and has to match it to its equivalent lower

case letter. The names of the letters are also taught at the same time.

6 Components

There are four major components used as teaching aids in *Way in*:

Way in A Pupil's Book

This book is divided into fifteen units. Each unit is divided further into two presentation pages in full colour and two workpages in black and white.

(i) The presentation pages provide the stimulus for the oral presentation of the language.
(ii) The workpages lay the foundation for early reading and writing skills. The language presented orally is consolidated through exercises such as matching pictures to pictures/words, drawing and colouring pictures according to instructions and completing puzzles.

Way in B Pupil's Book

This is also divided into fifteen units and follows the same pattern as *Way in A*.

Way in Teacher's Guide

This is a detailed guide to the course material and provides all the information required for the teaching of the course. The methodology for teaching the four language skills is set out. Each lesson is split up into a number of steps.

Way in Cassette

The cassette has the recording of the 30 songs and rhymes from *Way in*. These are very simple for the children to listen to and learn. They are based on the vocabulary and the sentence patterns presented in the course. The words are given at the back of the Pupil's Books and in the lesson notes in the Teacher's Guide.

The teacher may want to supplement *Way in* with other material, e.g. *Ladybird* books, *Bonanza*, *It's fun to write*. *Bonanza* is a collection of language games and picture cards for very young children. *It's fun to write* is a handwriting book for young children. In the teaching notes throughout *Way in* there are suggestions as to where these materials can be used effectively.

7 Reading

All methods of teaching reading work. Three factors play an important part: the teacher, the material, and the children's knowledge.

The teacher herself has an important role. She has to be patient and encourage the children. This will make learning to read easy for them and they will be relaxed and enjoy the tasks set. The teacher should also know what interests her particular children. The reading material must be stimulating and make sense to them. The children themselves must be able to understand and speak some English, otherwise they may say the words and yet not understand them. This is not reading.

7.1 Pre-reading

The first stage of reading is the pre-reading stage. At this point the children are learning to understand and to speak the language. This period is important because a foundation in aural, oral, visual and motor abilities has to be laid.

Visual abilities

The importance of visual abilities to the reading process cannot be overestimated. The children must learn to tell the difference between different shapes, e.g. letter and word shapes. If they can do this then they are ready to learn to read. To prepare them for this stage the teacher can give them tasks which develop this skill. For example:

a The completion of jigsaw puzzles. This develops skill in matching.
b Playing Snap, picture dominoes, etc. This also aids matching.
c Tracing, drawing, colouring, joining dots to form pictures, completing outline drawings. These all aid visual discrimination and motor control. Motor control refers to the child's ability to control movements of the hand (up and down, right to left,

left to right and circular) so that pencil marks are firm, not shaky.
d Selecting identical pictures from groups of similar pictures.
e Sorting shapes, pictures, objects into boxes.
f Playing Kim's Game. This is a game in which children have a limited time in which to try to memorize a number of objects. Show five objects to the class one by one, for several seconds each. (They must know the names of them in English.) Let the children see the objects together for a few seconds and tell them to try to remember them. Cover up the objects with a cloth. Now tell the children to work in pairs and tell their friend what they remembered. Go around the class asking each pair for the names of the objects.

Visual memory

In order to read the children must see the words and then be able to recognize them. This means that they have to memorize words. Some children have difficulty in remembering words. It is necessary therefore to repeat the words many times. In *Way in* this is done through reading games and activities so that repetition is ensured but boredom avoided. The following tasks aid development of visual memory.

a Completing drawings of common objects with parts missing, e.g. a face, a table.
b Drawing from memory a shape, e.g. a square or a triangle that the children have been shown.
c Tracing letters or words and copying them.

Left to right direction

The children must learn to move their eyes as smoothly as possible along a line from left to right. They must be able to do this not only because English is written from left to right, but because it helps in the recognition of letters which are inversions of other letters, e.g. b and d, n and u. The pattern practice in *Way in A* aids this. Other activities which aid left to right directionality are:

a Following pictures in a left to right sequence.
b Sorting action pictures into the correct left–right sequence.
c Doing simple mazes, tracing a trail from left to right.

d Tracing and colouring letters.
e Copying words.

Auditory abilities

The first contact that the children have with the English language is through hearing it spoken. If the child cannot hear properly or if the teacher's speech itself is not clear, then the child's language development will be delayed. If children are unable to tell the difference between, for example, bag and back, if they confuse the sounds, the children will reproduce the confusion in their own speech. This, in the first instance, will result in a breakdown of communication with others. To hear sounds accurately is important in learning to read. The sound of a word is associated with the printed word. Hearing the language and the language sounds clearly helps reading in the following ways. It builds up vocabulary. It helps the memorization of words, and therefore it helps the child to recognize the printed word. It helps the child to hear the particular letter sounds. This ensures that they can 'attack' new words that they meet. Development in reading is dependent on just that. The following activities aid auditory discrimination:

a The game of 'I spy'. In this game children try to guess an object beginning with a certain letter. The teacher says 'I spy with my little eye something beginning with (F)'. The children then have to guess the object e.g. floor, foot. The child who guesses correctly is the winner and can then think of an object and say 'I spy . . . .'
b Listening for sounds inside and outside the classroom.
c Singing songs and rhymes.
d Listening to rhyming words.
e Obeying oral instructions, e.g. 'Touch your toes.'
f Learning the letter sounds of the alphabet.
g Clapping back a rhythm that you tap for them.

All these activities are merely guidelines. They are listed here to help the teacher to check that the children are progressing and that they have reached a certain stage where they can learn to read. In *Way in* a variety of these activities have been selected. Listening exercises, for example, are included throughout both *Way in A* and *Way in B*.

7.2 *Way in*'s approach to reading

As every method of reading works the question is which one to choose. *Way in* uses a combination of two popular methods.

'Look and Say'

The 'Look and Say' approach to reading is where the child looks at the print on a flashcard and says the word. Pictures and objects are used to convey the meaning, e.g. a picture of a cat is shown and then the flashcard with 'cat' on it. The child looks at it and repeats 'cat' after the teacher. The child begins to understand that the print represents the spoken word. Eventually, after seeing the flashcard several times and saying the word the child comes to recognize the word and its meaning. The advantage of the 'Look and Say' method is that it gives the opportunity for the children to build up a large vocabulary quite quickly. This increases their confidence. Secondly, the vocabulary learnt is related to language that the children know. It is, therefore, instantly meaningful to them. Thirdly, as the English language is irregular, words can be learnt that do not fit into a particular pattern, e.g. turtle, elephant. A disadvantage that has been put forward is that the child does not pay attention to the individual letters and so might develop careless reading habits. The teacher can however combat this problem by using the phonic approach to complement the 'Look and Say'.

Phonics

The phonic approach focuses on the sound of words. In the first stage the teacher asks the children to give other sounds which begin with the sound they are learning. For example, if they are learning 'buh' for 'b', the children might say 'ball' and 'bat'. At this stage only words with regular phonic patterns are presented. Understanding of the words is essential in this approach too. One advantage of the phonic approach is that children can 'attack' a new word by sounding out the letters and pronouncing it. For example, if they can read 'cat' and 'dog' then, the theory runs, they can read 'cog'. This makes them independent of the teacher. They do not have to ask what the word sounds like.

A second advantage is that the child pays attention

to individual letters. This aids spelling and emphasizes the left to right direction. The disadvantage of the phonic approach is that English is irregular. It is impossible to teach children to read using this approach only. Soon words like 'table', 'what', etc. have to be introduced and the 'Look and Say' method adopted. To rely totally on the phonic method is to restrict vocabulary growth.

A further criticism of the phonic method is that the sounding of individual letters does not give the sound of the original word. For example, a child sounding out 't-a-p' could produce 'tapper'. Learning to read is a very complex task, demanding a wide variety of abilities and skills. Because of this *Way in* follows a combined approach using both 'Look and Say' and the phonic method.

Way in A begins with the 'Look and Say' method. This ensures that the children learn to read words they have learnt orally. They are therefore meaningful to them. The phonic approach complements the 'Look and Say' method from Unit 2 onwards in *Way in A*. Here the sounds of the initial letters of words are emphasized and a variety of phonic activities (e.g. I spy) are included in the lesson notes.

The text in *Way in*

The text that appears on the page in the Pupil's Book has two purposes. For the teacher and parent it shows clearly what language is being taught. The illustrations convey the meaning but the text ensures that the teacher knows exactly what words are to be presented. Secondly, having the text on the page helps word recognition. Although the children are not expected to read the text in the early stages of *Way in A* they can associate the language that they hear and produce with the marks on the paper. Then, gradually, throughout *Way in A* when flashcards are introduced the children can match the cards to the words and understand their meaning. By the end of *Way in A* the children should be able to read the text. They copy the words and sentences that they have seen and this aids their reading skill as well as their writing skill.

7.3 Progress in reading

Children develop at different rates. Some children will learn to read quickly, others will be slower. In *Way in A* the foundation for the first stages of learning to read is made in the early units. The children learn to:

a match picture to picture plus word.
b match picture to picture to word.
c read the word.

At the beginning of *Way in A* the child should be able to match a picture to the same picture. This stage should be reached before starting the course. At the end of *Way in A* the children are expected to read individual words i.e. to pronounce them and to know their meaning. At the end of *Way in B* the children should be able to read short, simple sentences and match them to the correct pictures.

7.4 Teaching reading

a Revise the vocabulary item or sentence orally. Demonstrate the meaning when saying it, e.g. hold up a ball and say 'ball'.
b Ask the class to repeat the item after you.
c Hold up the flashcard with 'ball' printed on it.
d Show the card and say 'ball'.
e Ensure that the children look at the card and say 'ball'. They can repeat it a few times.
f Teach other new words in the same way e.g. 'kite', 'bird'.
g Write up 'ball', 'kite' and 'bird' on the board. Hold up a card with one of the words written on it and ask for a child to come out and match it to the word written on the board. Do the same for the other items. Say the word when the child matches it.
h Finally, place the objects – ball, kite, picture of a bird, on the table. Hold up a flashcard and ask if a child can come out and match the flashcard to the object. Do not name a particular child.

Other reading activities in the form of games will be given in the lesson notes.
Two factors are essential to ensure success:

a The child must have ample practice at each stage.
b Each child must learn at his or her own pace.

8 Writing

Children need to be helped to write fluently and legibly. They must not be left alone to discover how to write for themselves, otherwise they will invent their own ways of making letter shapes. Some children may be successful, others will develop slow and clumsy movements. Eventually their writing will be difficult to read. Careful training, particularly when the roman alphabet is foreign to them, is essential.

8.1 Pre-writing

Handwriting is primarily physical. In order to be able to write the child needs to achieve finger control and coordinate hand and eye movements. The following activities encourage the necessary skills:

a Tracing or copying patterns in sand or on paper.
b Colouring in pictures.
c Joining dot to dot pictures.
d Jigsaw puzzles.
e Free drawing.
f Sorting shapes, little toys and bricks into boxes.
g Cutting out with scissors.
h Tracing line drawings.
i Modelling in clay or plasticine.
j Tracing mazes.
k Threading beads.

If children can perform these tasks with sufficient hand–eye coordination, if they can see patterns in their work and are aware of direction (left–right) then they are ready to learn to write.
From the above list it is clear that there is an overlap with the abilities required for reading. Reading and writing are skills that are interwoven. Thus visual abilities, visual memory, left to right directionality and auditory abilities aid the development of both reading and writing.

8.2 Teaching writing

Formation of letter shape
The teacher, from the beginning, has to train the children to complete the letters properly and form them carefully.

a Write the letter on the board. Ask the children what shape it looks like.
b Trace the letter in the air, then on desks and then on friends' backs.
c Ask the children to trace the letter over the one in their books with their forefingers.

Posture
Posture is important. The children must sit up straight at a desk or table and hold their pencils correctly between their forefinger and thumb. The paper has to be placed straight in front of the child.

Dot joining
Now ask them to trace over the letter with their pencils and join up the dots carefully. Check their work. At this point work with each child individually, showing them on their own page how to form letters. This one to one teaching is very important.

Rules for writing independently
Finally the children can write a line of letters on their own underneath. Insist that

a they start and finish in the correct space.
b that all upward and downward strokes be of the same length.
c the letters be in proportion and all the same size.
d the children use the writing line to write on.
e some letters are formed from left to right, e.g. n, and some from right to left, e.g. o. The children must be trained to form them in the correct way.
f when writing similar letter shapes, e.g. h and n, c and o, the difference between them has to be evident.

8.3 Writing for homework

Should the children need more practice they can write five examples of a letter or letters for their homework in their exercise books. If the above points are put into practice then this will ensure that the children develop good clear handwriting.

8.4 Writing in *Way in*

The children are taught how to form letters and

write words and sentences in *Way in*. The script they learn is printing. This provides a basis for the children to proceed to cursive, i.e. joined up writing. After *Way in* you might wish to consolidate the children's handwriting skills by using *It's fun to write*. This gives very thorough practice in letter formation and introduces the beginning stages of cursive writing.

9 Teaching procedures for *Way in*

This section deals with important classroom techniques and sets out suggested procedures for teaching *Way in*. It is intended for the beginning teacher but it is also of help to those teachers who are experienced with the very young beginner.

9.1 Guidelines to the teacher

The teacher is extremely important in the teaching of young children. She encourages her class and conveys a positive attitude to learning. In carrying out this task here are some points to remember:

a Treat all children equally. Give every child the opportunity to answer.

b Vary the pace of the lesson. Never stick rigidly to a pattern as the children's interest needs to be stimulated and the concentration span of young children is short. Remember that their attention lasts only between 10–15 minutes. It is essential that the children do not get bored.

c Do teach language 'by the way'. When playing games outside you can bring in English expressions and instructions naturally. And when doing creative activities, e.g. drawing pictures, you could say for example 'Show me the small one' and indicate what you mean. This was how the children learnt their first language after all.

d Fluency in English at this stage is more important than accuracy. Constant correction hinders fluency as well as undermining confidence. Do not interrupt a child who makes a mistake, merely repeat the word later, correctly. Accuracy in pronunciation is a skill most children acquire quickly. They are excellent imitators so they can achieve near native pronunciation (if given the model). This leads to increased confidence and a strong motivation to master the language.

e When asking a question pause and give the children time to think of the answer. Give every child the opportunity to answer.

f At the beginning of the course ask for volunteers to answer questions or come out and participate actively. Do not ask specific children as some may not have sufficient confidence at first.

g Do make the classroom a bright, lively and interesting place. Label the various things in it, e.g. the door, window, ceiling, chair and table. Draw attention to the labels from time to time and change them occasionally. New labels and posters will stimulate and sustain the children's interest in the things around them. Number, colour and alphabet posters can be displayed as well as the children's own work. When labelling avoid capital letters until the children learn them in *Way in B*.

h To teach reading you need to use flashcards. To make a flashcard:

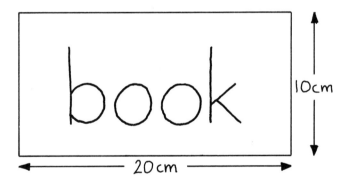

(i) Take a piece of white card and cut a piece 20cm × 10cm. If the word is particularly long e.g. elephant, clearly you will have to make the card longer.

(ii) Draw a line across the card in pencil first. Draw it just below the middle.

(iii) Write the word in pencil first, making sure that each letter is in proportion. Use lower case letters.

(iv) Go over it in felt tip or ink.

Use flashcards in games, e.g. Bingo, which is described in Units 5 and 13 of *Way in A*. See also section 7.3 Reading.

i The furniture arrangement is important. If possible have the desks grouped, as this saves time during the lesson. Alternatively, for the oral presentation, seat the children (and yourself) on the floor. You can do this for games too. This will make for a relaxed atmosphere.

j Finally, always keep the children interested through the songs, games and activities so that they find it a pleasure to learn. The success of the course depends on you and success means that the children look forward to learning English.

9.2 Use of the mother tongue

The use of the mother tongue in teaching English is often an area of debate. When teaching very young children it is important to give them a feeling of security and hearing their mother tongue spoken ensures confidence in the situation. From this base the teacher can introduce more and more English. In *Way in* Teacher's Guide the teacher is advised when to use the mother tongue (which is referred to as L1) and when to use English. The English sentences are always in italics, e.g. *What's this?* The children's first language should always be used to set the scene for the lessons, to discuss what is happening in the illustrations. Instructions at the beginning of this course will also be in the first language. Gradually, however, introduce simple English instructions side by side with their mother tongue and accompany them with simple gestures, e.g. 'Come here'. Very soon the children will understand the instruction in English on its own and be able to carry out the instruction. Do not expect them to produce these sentences themselves though.

9.3 Teaching meaning

It is essential that the children understand what the vocabulary items and the sentences that they learn mean. The following techniques can be used.

a Point to, or show the object (e.g. a kite), or show a picture of an object.
b Draw a picture of the object on the board.
c Do the action, e.g. jump.
d Mime or use gestures, e.g. I can swim.
e Explain in the mother tongue.

9.4 Chorus work

a Use chorus work in oral practice periods. This gives every child the opportunity to imitate and repeat. Small children enjoy this.

b Divide the class into chorus groups. The number of groups depends on the size of the class. Call them by a number, a colour, or a *Way in* character. By dividing them into groups you can hear if the children are repeating the sentences correctly. This is the point where you may correct their pronunciation.

c Speak clearly. This helps the children to imitate properly.

d Use gestures to accompany the sentences. For example, with 'I can jump', you can jump.

e Listen to the children carefully and correct their mistakes. You may need to repeat the vocabulary item or sentence before they chorus it again.

f Should the children become too noisy stop them. Tell them to begin more quietly. If you lower your voice they will imitate this too.

g Be aware of the children's attention span. Stop when they have had enough practice. Change to another activity.

h In *Way in* most oral practice is first done in chorus work before changing to games and other activities. Chorus work gives the children confidence. Only you can judge when it is time for you to ask individual children to say the sentences. This will be *after* sufficient chorus work.

i Use the puppets in oral work.

9.5 Songs and rhymes

The following method for teaching the songs and rhymes is suggested:

a Play the entire song or rhyme first and you sing or say the words too.
b Play it again, still joining in with the words and the whole class can clap to it.
c Play it and encourage the children to join in with the words and actions.

A song or rhyme is taught in the second and third lesson of every unit. They can also be used for revision at the beginning of a lesson too.

List of recommended visual aids to make

1 A set of cards of all the lower case letters of the alphabet. A duplicate set for playing games.

2 A set of cards for all the capital letters. A duplicate set for playing games.

3 A set of cards coloured in: blue, black, brown, green, grey, red, yellow, white.

4 Where flashcards are used in a lesson these will be listed in the Preparation step for that lesson. Below is a list of all the flashcards needed during the course.
Flashcards for all the nouns:

apple	brother	elephant	hand	mother	tail
balloon	brown	eye	hat	mouse	trumpet
bees	cake(s)	family	head	nose	TV
bike	camera	father	hen(s)	octopus	umbrella
bird	cat	fire	house	plane	white
black	chair	fish	ice cream	radio	window
blue	chocolate	flags	kite	red	yellow
boat	door	floor	ladder	shells	zebra
book	drum	green	leg	sister	
box	ear	grey	lemons	stars	
bread	egg	guitar	man	table	

Flashcards for the following sentences:

I can jump.	I'm on the chair.	That's my boat.
I can swim.	I'm in the box.	I like red.
I can fly.	I'm big.	I like yellow.
I can run.	I'm little.	I can see a hand.
I'm under the table.	That's my house.	I can see a man.

5 Cards for practising numbers:
 a 'Number dominoes' (like those in Units 4 and 8 of the Pupil's Book) for all the numbers up to ten.
 b Flashcards with the number words on them 'one', etc. for all numbers up to ten.

6 The following can be made in class:
 a An alphabet frieze.
 b A number frieze.
 c A colour book (see Unit 3, Lesson 3).

Way in A: Language Summary

Unit 1	Hello. I'm . . .	door window	floor	
Unit 2	Look. That's a . . .	a balloon a bird	a kite a ladder	a plane a tree
Unit 3	Colour. I'm . . .	blue green	red yellow	
Unit 4	1 one 2 two 3 three 4 four			
Unit 5	That's a . . .	a boat an elephant	a fire a fish	
Unit 6	What's this?	an ear an eye a hand	a head a leg a nose	a tail
Unit 7	I have a . . .	an apple a book	a cat a mouse	an octopus
Unit 8	5 five 6 six 7 seven 8 eight	an egg a zebra		
Unit 9	What's this?	a radio a T.V.		
Unit 10	It's . . .	black brown	grey white	
Unit 11	I like . . . I don't like . . .	bread cake	chocolate ice cream	an umbrella
Unit 12	It's in the . . . Draw a . . .	a box an egg	a hat	

Unit 13	9 nine . 10 ten		
Unit 14	It's on the . . . Where's the . . . ? I'm on the . . .	a cake a chair	a table
Unit 15	Happy birthday I'm (four).		

Way in B: Language Summary

Unit 1	Hallo. My name's . . . What's your name?		
Unit 2	This is (Pam).		
Unit 3	I can . . .	fly jump	run swim
Unit 4	One hen. Two eggs. Three lemons. Four cakes.		
Unit 5	Where's . . . ? Here I am. I'm on the . . . I'm under the . . .		
Unit 6	I'm big. It's little.		
Unit 7	I have a . . . . . . and a . . .	a camera a drum	a guitar a trumpet
Unit 8	Is it a . . . ? Yes. No.		
Unit 9	That's my . . .	a bike a house	
Unit 10	Five shells. Six flags. Seven stars.		
Unit 11	That's my . . .	brother father	mother sister
Unit 12	This is your . . .	family	

Unit 13	I like red.	blue green	yellow
Unit 14	Eight bees. Nine bees. Ten bees.		
Unit 15	I can see . . . Goodbye.	a man	

Way in A: **Unit 1**

LESSON 1

New language	Known language
Hallo.	
I'm . . .	
door	
window	

Preparation
- Make three labels: 'door', 'floor', 'window'. Put them on the places.

- Prepare enough pieces of plain paper for each child for drawing.

- Have the Drago and Otto puppets ready to use.

Presentation
- (L1) Explain to the class that you are going to greet them in English and that they have to repeat the greeting after you. Say *Hallo*. Say it again and ask the class to repeat it. Do this several times. Quickly divide the class into small groups (three or four children in each group) and tell them to say *Hallo* to each other.

- (L1) Now explain that you are going to introduce yourself in English and everyone must listen carefully. Point to yourself and say *I'm . . . .* Repeat this. Do not ask the children to introduce themselves yet.

PB page 2
- (L1) Here are Drago and Otto introducing themselves. Ask the children what animals they can see in the picture. (L1) Explain that Drago and Otto are saying hallo.
(L1) Tell them to look at the dragon. They are all going to pretend they are Drago. Say *I'm Drago*. Say it a few times. Let the children repeat it after you. (L1) Tell them to look at the octopus. They will now pretend to be the octopus. Say *I'm Otto*. Say it a few times and let the children repeat it after you.

Practice
- Show the class the puppets, Drago and Otto. Hold up Drago and say *I'm Drago* and let the children repeat it after you. Now hold up the Otto puppet and say *I'm Otto*. Let the children hold up their own puppets and repeat *I'm Otto*.

- Point to yourself and say *I'm . . . .* (L1) Explain to the children that they can say who they are in turn. Ask for individual volunteers to stand up and say *I'm . . . .* Do not force anyone.

- Quickly divide the class up into small groups. Have about six children in each group. Give them each a number and when working in groups, begin with group 1, then group 2 and so on. Then you can vary the order and perhaps start with group 4 for a change.

- Hold up your Drago puppet and say *I'm Drago*. Group 1 repeats it after you. Say it again and group 2 repeats it and so on. Now hold up the Otto puppet and do the same.

- Now the children all say *I'm (name)*. Do not force any of them. Ask for volunteers to say who they are.

Activities
- (L1) Explain to the children that they can draw either Drago or Otto. Give out the paper. Go around when the children are working and praise and encourage them. When they have finished put all the drawings up on the classroom wall.

- (L1) Tell the children that they are going to learn a game. Point to the door and say *door*. Say it several times. Point to the window and say *window* several times. Now explain that you are going to say 'window' or 'door' and that they must point to the right place when you do, otherwise they are out. Begin the game. Say *door*. The last child to point to the door is out. Now say *window*. Quicken the pace and continue the game until one child only is left. She or he is the winner.

LESSON 2

New language	Known language
floor	Hallo
	I'm . . .

Preparation
- Have the Tubs and Belinda puppets ready to use.

Revision
- Hold up the Drago puppet and say *I'm Drago*. Let the children do the same holding their puppets. Hold up the Otto puppet and say *I'm Otto* and the children do the same.

- (L1) Ask if any of the children would now like to say who they are. Encourage them to do so but do not force them.

PB page 3
- The elephant is saying who she is, (she's Belinda), and the turtle is saying who he is, (he's Tubs). (L1) Explain that they are friends of Drago and Otto and that they have lots of adventures together. (L1) Tell the children to look at Tubs and they are all going to pretend to be him. Say *I'm Tubs*. Let the children look at the picture and repeat *I'm Tubs* after you. Do this several times. Now they can look at the elephant. They are going to pretend that they are Belinda. Say *I'm Belinda* and let the children look at the picture and say the sentence after you. Do this a few times.

Practice
- (L1) Tell the children to hold up their Tubs puppet. Hold up yours and say *I'm Tubs*. Divide the children up into their groups, making sure that there are at least three groups, and let each group repeat the sentence after you.

- (L1) Now ask if any child wants to come out with the puppets and say the sentences. Again, encourage them but do not force them.

PB page 4 Ex. 1
- (L1) Explain to the children that the four friends are saying who they are. (L1) Tell them that you are going to pretend to be the different animals and that you are going to say *I'm . . . .* If the animal on the page is the same as the name that you say, then they must put a tick (✓) in the box. Draw a tick on the board. For example, if the picture on the page is Drago and you say *I'm Drago* then they have to put a tick: ✓. If the picture is Belinda and you say *I'm Drago*, then they must put a cross in

the box: ✗. Do the first example with the class.

1) I'm Tubs.
2) I'm Asterix.
3) I'm Belinda.
4) I'm Otto.

Repeat the sentence several times to give the children the opportunity to decide if it is right or wrong. At the end go over the whole activity with the class. Praise them when they get the right answer.

Activity
● Play the game from the previous lesson again. Say *door* and then *window* and the children have to point to the right object. (L1) Now explain that you are going to include another word – 'floor'. Point to the floor and say *floor*. Say it several times. Now play the game again using the three words. The last child to point is out. The winner is the one child remaining 'in'.

Song
● If there is time, play the song that the children are going to learn in the next lesson.

LESSON 3

New language	Known language
Hallo	window
I'm . . .	floor
door	

Revision
● Say *Hallo* to the class and encourage them to reply. Point to yourself and say *I'm . . . .* Encourage individual children to say who they are. (L1) Divide them into pairs and explain that they must greet one another and say who they are. They say *Hallo. I'm . . . .*

PB page 5
Ex. 2
● (L1) Explain to the children that they must draw in their own eyes, nose and mouth on the outline head and colour it in. If the children can write their own names in roman script let them. Otherwise they can write their names in their own language.

PB page 5
Ex. 3
● (L1) Tell the children that Otto, Drago and Tubs have been walking on the sand. What happens when you walk on sand? Here are three trails to follow. Tracing them over will help develop the children's hand and eye coordination and encourage left to right directionality. (L1) First tell them to put their forefinger at the beginning of the first trail – on the left – and trace over it. They can trace over the next two trails. Make sure that they are all starting on the left.

● (L1) Now explain that they can take their pencils (ordinary pencils, not too fat) and join up the dotted trails from left to right. Check their posture and ensure that their books are straight in front of them. Go around when the children are joining the dots and help the children who have difficulty.

Song
● Tell the class that you have a song for them to learn. Play the entire song through

first. Then play the first verse and sing the words. Let the class clap or hum to it. Play the first verse again and encourage the children to join in and sing it. You could then divide the class up and let each group be a different character and sing that part, e.g. the Drago group sings 'I'm Drago', etc. Play the second and third verses and teach them in the same way.

1   I'm Belinda.
    I'm Tubs.
    I'm Belinda.
    I'm Tubs.
    I'm Belinda.
    I'm Tubs.
    Hallo, hallo, hallo.

2   I'm Otto.
    I'm Drago.
    I'm Otto.
    I'm Drago.
    I'm Otto.
    I'm Drago.
    Hallo, hallo, hallo.

3   I'm Belinda.
    I'm Tubs.
    I'm Belinda.
    I'm Tubs.
    I'm Otto.
    I'm Drago.
    Hallo, hallo, hallo.
    Hallo, hallo, hallo.

LESSON 1

New language	Known language
Look.	
a balloon	
a kite	
a bird	

Preparation
- Draw pictures on the board of a balloon, a bird, and a kite.
- Make two letter cards with 'b' and 'k' on them.

Presentation
- Point to the balloon on the board and say *a balloon*. Say it several times. Let the children look at the balloon and say 'a balloon' after you. Divide them into their groups and let each group repeat it after you. Do the same with 'kite' and 'bird'.

- Play 'Jumping the line'. Find an open area in the classroom or play the game outside. Draw a line in chalk on the floor and tell the class that one side is 'true' and the other is 'false'. (L1) Explain that you are going to point to a picture on the board and say, e.g. *a bird*. If it is true, if it *is* a picture of a bird, then they must jump to the 'true' side of the line. If it is *not* a bird, then they must jump to the 'false' side. If a child makes a mistake then he or she is out. The game ends when all the players except one are out. That player is the winner.

PB page 6
- Drago and Tubs have found a hot air balloon. They decide to go up in it. (L1) Tell the children to look at the top picture and explain what Drago is saying. Then say *Look. A balloon.* Let the children repeat this after you. Divide them up into their groups and let group 1 repeat it after you, then group 2, etc.

- (L1) Ask the class to look at the bottom picture. Drago and Tubs are leaning out of the balloon in excitement as they fly past a kite and a bird. Ask them to look at the kite. Say *A kite.* Say it a few times. Let the children look at it and repeat it after you. Divide the class up into their groups and let them repeat it after you. Do this a few times. Let them repeat it in their groups. Do the same with *A bird*.

Practice
- (L1) Ask the children to put their Drago and Tubs puppets on their fingers: one on each hand. Explain that you are all going to act out the story. Hold up your Drago puppet and say *Look. A balloon.* Let group 1 say it after you, then group 2, etc. Hold up your Drago puppet again and say *A kite.* Each group can repeat it. Finally hold up the Tubs puppet and say *A bird.* Let the groups in turn repeat it after you.

- (L1) Now ask if any child would like to come out with the puppets and act out the story. Let as many as would like to come out.

A–Z
- (L1) Explain to the children that they are going to learn some letters. Letters make up words and they are going to learn them in order to play games with them. Say that letters have sounds *and* names. At the moment, however, they will learn just the sounds. First say *balloon* and point to the balloon. Emphasize the initial sound /b/ and write 'b' on the board. Point to the kite and say *kite*. Emphasize the initial sound

/k/ and write 'k' on the board. Point to each sound and pronounce it. Let the children pronounce each one after you while looking at the correct letter. Do this a few times. Make sure that you are always pointing to the letter and that the children are looking at the one that you are pronouncing.

- (L1) Tell the children that you are going to say one of the sounds and that you want someone to come up and point to the right letter. Do this a few times with different children but only the ones who volunteer.

- Now show the class the two letter cards 'b' and 'k'. (L1) Tell them that you want two children to come up and match the cards to the right letters on the board. When they come up encourage them to say the sound as well but do not force them. (L1) Finally tell the children that you are going to trace one of the letters, either 'b' or 'k' and that they have to guess which one it is. Do this a few times.

LESSON 2

New language	Known language
That's a . . .	
a plane	
a tree	
a ladder	

Preparation

- Make alphabet cards for 'l' and 't'.

- Draw a plane, a tree, and a ladder on the board.

Presentation

- Point to the tree on the board and say *a tree*. The class repeats this after you. Point to the plane and say *a plane*. Let the children repeat it. Do this several times with both pictures. Point to the ladder and say *a ladder*. Say it a few times and let the children repeat it after you. Divide the class into their groups to repeat each word.

- Divide the class into two teams, A and B. (L1) Explain to the class that you are going to say one of the words, tree, ladder or plane, and one child from each team has to come out and point to the correct picture. If they are right then they get a point. Say *a tree* and ask for a child from team A to come out. Then say *a ladder* and ask for someone from team B to come out and so on.

- Point to the tree on the board and say *That's a tree*. Say it a few times. (L1) Check that the children understand the meaning of the sentence. Say it again and let them repeat it after you. Divide the class up into groups to repeat it. (L1) Explain that you don't necessarily have to point when you say 'That's'.

PB page 7

- Drago and Tubs have leaned too far out of the balloon and have fallen out. They land in a tree and Belinda helps them by putting a ladder up for them. (L1) Tell the class to look at the top picture. Tubs is looking at a plane. Say *That's a plane*. The children look at the picture and say *That's a plane*. Divide the class into their groups to repeat it. (L1) Tell them to look at Drago pointing to the tree. Say *That's a tree*. Let the class repeat it after you. Say it again and then group 1 repeats it after you, group 2 and so on. Now they can look at the ladder. Say *That's a ladder.* Say it a few times. Let the class repeat it after you all together, then in groups.

Practice • (L1) Tell the class that they are going to pretend to be Drago and Tubs. Pretend to be Tubs, point to the plane on the board and say *That's a plane.* Groups repeat it after you in turn. Pretend to be Drago and say *That's a tree* and point to the tree on the board. Let group 1 repeat it after you and then the other groups in turn. Pretend to be Drago and point to the ladder on the board. Say *That's a ladder.* Groups repeat it after you, holding their Drago puppets.

• (L1) Ask if any children wish to come out and act or mime the whole story. One child can be Drago, another Tubs and a third Belinda.

A–Z • Point to the picture of the ladder on the board and say *ladder.* Emphasize the initial sound /l/. Write 'l' on the board. Point to the tree and say *tree.* Say the sound /t/ and write 't' on the board. Point to each of them and say their sound. Do this a few times and let the children repeat them after you. Make sure that you are always pointing to the letter and that the children are looking at the one that they are pronouncing.

• (L1) Tell them that you are now going to say one of the sounds and that you want someone to come up and point to the right letter. Do this with a few children.

• Show the class the two letter cards with 'l' and 't' on them. Tell the class that you want two children to come up and match the cards to the right letters on the board. When they come up, ask them if they can say the sound as well but do not force them.

PB page 8 Ex. 1 • (L1) Explain to the class that they are going to have to listen very carefully. You are going to say a word and if that word is the same as the picture then they must put a tick in the box. If the word is *not* the same as the picture then they must put a cross. Do the first example with the whole class.

1) Belinda
2) a plane
3) a tree
4) a ladder
5) a kite
6) a bird

Always say the word several times so that the children have the opportunity to decide if it is right or wrong. Go around to check on their work. Go over the exercise with the whole class.

PB page 8 Ex. 2 • First draw the shape 'n' on the board. (L1) Then tell the children to look at you while you draw the shape in the air with your finger. Stand with your back to the class while you do it. Let them copy you, also using their forefingers. They can trace the shape on their desks, on their friends' backs, etc. Then they can trace over the shapes on the page with their forefingers. Tell the class that they can join the dots and then colour in the picture. Go around and help those who have problems. Remind them to sit properly and hold their pencils correctly. Their books should be straight in front of them.

Song
- If there is time let the children sit and listen to the song that they are going to learn in the next lesson.

LESSON 3

New language	Known language
	a ladder
	a tree

Preparation
- Draw a picture of a tree and a ladder on the board.

**PB page 9
Ex. 3**
- First draw a 'u' shape on the board. The children have to look carefully at it. Trace the shape in the air. Let them copy you using their forefingers. They can trace it in the air, on their friends' backs, and on their desks. Tell them to sit properly and put their books straight in front of them.

- (L1) Ask them what Belinda is doing at the top of page 9. She is going to have a drink from the cups on the table. (L1) Tell them that they can now trace over the cups, the dotted outline, with their forefinger. Finally they can join the dots together with their pencils. Go around and help individual children.

**PB page 9
Ex. 4**
- Write the letters b, k, t, and 1 on the board several times. Join one of the 'b's to another. (L1) Explain to the children that you want a volunteer to come up and join another 'b' to that one. Ask another child to come up. When all the 'b's have been joined ask for volunteers to join the 't's and so on.

- (L1) Explain that Otto has a game for them. They must look at the letter outside the box and then look at the ones inside and find the odd letter out. Do the first example with the class. Go around and help individual children.

Song
- (L1) Explain to the children that they are now going to learn a song about the game that they played a few lessons ago. Play the first verse and sing it and do the actions while the children listen to it. Play the song again, sing the words and do the actions and encourage the children to join in with the actions at the same time. Play it again and they join in the actions and the words.

1 One little finger, tap, tap, tap!   *(Tap your finger on the table.)*
   One little finger, tap, tap, tap!
   Pointing at the ceiling,   *(Point at the ceiling.)*
   Pointing at the floor,   *(Point at the floor.)*
   Pointing at the window,   *(Point at the window.)*
   Pointing at the door!   *(Point at the door.)*
   One little finger, tap, tap, tap!
   One little finger, tap, tap, tap!

2 Two little fingers, tap, tap, tap!
   Two little fingers, tap, tap, tap!
   Pointing at the ceiling,
   Pointing at the floor,

Pointing at the window,
Pointing at the door!
Two little fingers, tap, tap, tap!
Two little fingers, tap, tap, tap!

LESSON 1

New language	Known language
green	I'm . . .
yellow	

Preparation
- Have ready a green card and a yellow card and two letter cards for 'g' and 'r'.

Presentation
- (L1) First check that the children are familiar with the names of the colours in their own language. Hold up the green and the yellow card and ask what the colour is. Now hold up the green card and say *green*. Repeat this a few times. Let the children repeat it after you. Do the same with the yellow card.

- (L1) Now explain that you are going to say a colour, and they must point to the right one. Hold up the two cards – one in each hand. Say *yellow* and then *green*. The children point to the correct card. Change the cards round and do it again.

- (L1) Ask for two children to come out to the front. Give each of them a coloured card. Explain that you are going to call out the name of the colour and then the class must say the name of the child who has the card of that colour. If the class are correct that child then holds up the card.

PB page 10
- (L1) Explain that Drago and Otto are saying what colour they are. Drago is saying that he is green. (L1) Tell the children to look at Drago and pretend to be him. Say *I'm green*. Say this a few times and let the children repeat it. (L1) Now ask the children to look at Otto. He's saying that he is yellow. Pretend that you are Otto and say *I'm yellow*. Let the children pretend and say *I'm yellow* several times.

Practice
- (L1) Tell the class to take out their Drago and Otto puppets. Divide the class into their groups. Hold up the Drago puppet and say *I'm green*. Group 1 repeats it after you, then group 2 and so on. Hold up the Otto puppet and say *I'm yellow*. Groups repeat it.

- (L1) Now ask if some children would like to come out with the puppets and say the sentence.

A–Z
- (L1) Explain to the children that they are going to learn two more letters. Point to the green card and say *green* and emphasize the initial sound /g/. Write 'g' on the board. Say /g/ and let the children repeat it after you. Now hold up the yellow card and say *yellow*. Emphasize the initial sound /j/ and write 'y' on the board. Say the sounds again while pointing at the letters. Let the children repeat the sounds after you. Do this a few times and make sure that you are pointing to the letter and the children are looking at the one that they are pronouncing.

- (L1) Explain to the class that you are going to say one of the sounds and that you want someone to come up and point to the correct letter. Do this a few times.

- Now show the children the 'g' and 'y' letter cards. (L1) Ask two of them to come up and match the cards to the letters on the board. Ask them if they can say the sound as well, but do not force them.

Activity
- Draw a tree, a ladder, a plane, a bird on the board. Divide the class into two teams. (L1) Explain to the children that you are going to call out an object and that a player from each team must then run and point to the right object. The first one to do so gets a point. Play until all the class have had a turn.

LESSON 2

New language	Known language
red	I'm . . .
blue	green
	yellow

Preparation
- Bring in four coloured cards, blue, red, green and yellow.

Revision
- Quickly hold up the green and the yellow cards, one in each hand. (L1) Tell the children that you will say a colour and they have to point to the correct card. Say *yellow* and then *green*.

Presentation
- Now teach the new colours, blue and red. (L1) First check that the class are familiar with those colours in their own language. Next hold up the blue card and say *blue*. Say it a few times and then let the children repeat it. Do the same with the red card.

- (L1) Now explain that, as before, you are going to say a colour and they must point to the right card. Say *blue* and then *red*. Change the cards around and do it again.

PB page 11
- Belinda is sunburnt and Tubs is freezing! Ask the children is Belinda usually red? Is Tubs usually blue? (L1) Explain that Belinda is saying that she is red and Tubs is saying that he is blue. (L1) Ask the children to look at Belinda. You are all going to pretend to be Belinda and be sunburnt. Say *I'm red*. Say this a few times and let the class repeat it after you. (L1) Now tell them to look at Tubs. They are all going to pretend to be Tubs. Say *I'm blue*. Say it several times and let the class repeat it after you.

Practice
- Divide the class into two groups only first. (L1) Tell one group that they are Belinda, group A, and one group that they are Tubs, group B. Say *I'm red*. Group A says *I'm red*. Then say *I'm blue*. Group B says *I'm blue*. Change the groups around so that group A is Tubs and group B is Belinda. Do this several times.

- Now divide the class into their usual groups. (L1) Tell them to choose to be either Belinda or Tubs and say *I'm red* or *I'm blue*. Group 1 begins, then group 2, and so on.

A–Z
- (L1) Explain to the class that they are going to learn one more letter sound. Point to the red card and say *red*. Emphasize the initial sound /r/ and write 'r' on the board. Say /r/ again and let the children repeat it after you. Write 'g' and 'y' up as well and point to the three letters and say the sounds.

- (L1) Tell the children that you are going to say a sound and they can come up and put a ring around the letter that has that sound. Do this several times with children who volunteer.

- Show them the letter card with 'r' on it and a volunteer comes up and finds the same letter on the board.

PB page 12
Ex. 1

- Tubs is being carried away by so many balloons. (L1) Ask the class what he is doing. (L1) Explain that they are going to join up the dots around the balloons. Follow the same steps as when teaching previous patterns. Draw a circle on the board in an anti-clockwise direction first. The children watch. Then, with your back to the class, trace the pattern in the air. Let the children imitate you using their forefinger. Make sure that they are making the movement anti-clockwise. Tell them to trace it on their desks, on their friends' backs, etc. At this point they can trace over the shapes on the page. Now the children can join the dots together using their pencils.

- When they have finished then they can colour the balloons in different colours. Go around and help each child.

PB page 12
Ex. 2

- (L1) Explain to the children that they are going to play a game with Tubs. They have to find the letter on the right which matches the letter on the left. Do the first example with the class. Go around and help any children who have problems.

Optional
activity

- (L1) Ask the children to select a colour and draw a character of their choice. You can display the pictures on the wall – all of them. Write the appropriate caption underneath each one, e.g. 'I'm Otto. I'm yellow.' From time to time draw the children's attention to the pictures and read the labels to them.

Rhyme

- Let the children listen to the rhyme that they will learn next lesson.

LESSON 3

New language	Known language
Colour.	green
	yellow
	blue
	red
	I'm . . .

Preparation

- Prepare 4 small coloured strips of paper for each child, one of each colour. Cut out plain paper circles – one for each child.

Revision

- Give out four coloured strips of paper to each child – a red, a blue, a yellow and a green. (L1) Explain to the children that you are going to say the name of a colour and that they must find the correct one and hold it up as quickly as possible. Have a trial run first. Say *red* and wait for all the children to hold up their red strips of paper. The last child to hold up the paper is out. Play until there is a winner.

PB page 13
Ex. 3

- (L1) Explain to the class that they are going to colour the shapes at the top of the page in different colours. Quickly draw a triangle, a square, a star and a circle on the board. (L1) Tell them that the triangle is to be coloured blue. Colour it in with a blue chalk and say *blue*. Do the same for the other shapes. (L1) Tell the children to colour the first one in. Go around and check that they are colouring it blue. Now they can do the second and so on. While the children are colouring in the shapes go to each child and point to the colours and give them the opportunity to tell you what the colours are. If any child is unable to do this you can point to each colour and say its name and the child can repeat it after you.

PB page 13
Ex. 4

- Teach the class the instruction *Colour*. Point to a child and say *Colour* and indicate that he or she must colour in something. (L1) Check that they have understood the instruction.

- Ask the class what Drago and his friends are doing. (L1) Explain that you are going to give them some instructions and they have to colour in the animals in the colour you say. They must listen very carefully.

  1) Colour Drago yellow.
  2) Colour Belinda blue.
  3) Colour Tubs green.
  4) Colour Otto red.

  Give the instructions two or three times. The children can colour the ball in whichever colour they like.

Optional activity

- Give out one paper circle to each child. (L1) Explain that they are balloons and that the children can colour them in one colour only, but they can choose which one.

- When they have finished you can put the blue 'balloons' in one corner, the red in another and so on. Then label the corners 'blue', 'red', 'yellow' and 'green'.

Rhyme

- Play the first verse of the rhyme. Let the class listen to it while you join in with the words. Play it again and encourage the children to join in with the words. Then play the second verse in the same way.

  1 Drago is green,
     Tubs is blue,
     Otto is yellow,
     What colour are you?

  2 Belinda is red,
     Tubs is blue,
     I am yellow,
     What colour are you?

Further suggestions

- Make colour books, one for each colour. This is an activity which can go on over several lessons. For this have four separate paper books. Write on the outside of each one 'a yellow book', 'a blue book', etc. (L1) Explain to the children that they can collect pictures at home and you will help them to stick a picture on each page. Underneath you may like to label the pictures, e.g. 'a green balloon'. Display the books in the classroom.

Way in A: **Unit 4**

LESSON 1

New language	Known language
one	
two	

Preparation

- Make a large card with ⃞1 ⃞• on it and another with ⃞2 ⃞: on it.

- Bring in four clothes pegs.

Presentation

- (L1) First check that the children are familiar with the numbers 1–4. Then hold up the card with 1 on it and say *one*. Repeat this a few times. Let the children repeat it after you. Do the same with 2. If you have a numbers frieze you may like to use that to teach the numbers.

- Now put one card in each hand. (L1) Explain that you are going to say a number and that the children must point to the correct card. When you have done this twice change the cards around.

- Give each child a number, 'one' or 'two'. (L1) Tell them that you are going to call out a number and when you say it all the children with that number must stand up. Say *one* and wait for all the children who are ones to stand. Now say *two*. Do this several times, quickening the pace.

PB page 14

- Drago is fishing in a pool, but he is catching crabs not fish! (L1) Tell the children to look at the first picture. Drago has caught one crab. Say *one*. Let the children repeat it after you. Do this a few times. When everyone is looking at the second picture say *two*. Let the children repeat it after you. Say it several times.

Practice

- (L1) Tell the class to pretend to be Drago. They are going fishing. Divide the class into their groups. (L1) Explain that first they'll fish the pool and catch one crab, and then they can fish again for a second one. Say *one* and, with the children looking at the top picture group 1 can repeat *one*, then group 2, and so on. (L1) Tell them to look at the bottom picture, and do the same for *two*.

- Ask if any of the class want to come out and act Drago fishing. Two children can come out and pretend to be the crabs that Drago catches. When he or she catches the first crab the rest of the class says *one* and when the second crab is caught the class can say *two*. You may like to do this a few times with different children.

A–Z

- Write all the letters that the children know on the blackboard: b, k, t, l, g, r, y. Point to each one and say its sound. Point to the letters at random and ask the class to say the sound all together when you do so.

- Now divide the class into two teams. (L1) Tell the children that you are going to say two letter sounds and then a player from team A has to say whether the sounds are the same or whether they are different. Then a child from team B has a turn. If the answer is correct the team gets a point. Give an example first. Say /b/ /b/. Is it the same or different? Then say /g/ /r/. Is it the same or different?

1) /k/ /k/; 2) /g/ /r/; 3) /b/ /j/; 4) /l/ /l/; 5) /t/ /k/.

Activity
- Play 'Dance of the Ostriches'. Go out into the playground or find an open area in the classroom. Divide the class into two teams. Select one child from each team and stand them facing each other. Attach a piece of paper showing a number, either 1 or 2, to the back of each child, using clothes pegs. Put the children's hands behind their backs. They have to dance round each other and try to see the number on the other child's back. Give a point to the first child to do so. Then it is the turn of the next children in the teams. The first team to get 3 points is the winner.

LESSON 2

New language	Known language
three	one
four	two

Preparation
- Have ready two large cards with 3 [:.] and 4 [::] on them.
- Bring in the cards with 1 [.] and 2 [:] on them.
- Bring in the letter cards 'f' and 't'.

Revision
- (L1) Tell the children that you are going to clap either once or twice. If you clap once they must say *one* and if you clap twice they must say *two*. Do this a few times.
- (L1) Now tell them that you are going to say *one* or *two* and they have to clap the correct number of times. Say *two*, then *one*. Quicken the pace and do it several times.

Presentation
- (L1) Check that the children know 'three' and 'four' in their own language. Then hold up the card with 3 on it and say *three*. Repeat this a few times. Let the children repeat it after you. Do the same for four.
- Put one card in each hand. (L1) Explain that, as before, you are going to say a number and they must point to the right card. When you have done this twice change the cards around and say the numbers again. Say *four*, then *three*.
- (L1) Now knock on the desk either three or four times and tell the children that they must tell you the right number. Play it again and include numbers one and two in the game.

PB page 15
- Drago is still fishing but the crabs decide to bite him. (L1) Ask the class to count the number of crabs in the top picture, then in the bottom picture. Have they ever been bitten by a crab? Tell them to look at the top picture again. Count the crabs. Say *one, two, three*. Do this a few times and let the children repeat the numbers after you. (L1) Tell the children to look at the bottom picture. Count the crabs again. Say *one, two, three, four*! Let the children repeat the numbers after you.

Practice
- (L1) Divide the class into their groups and tell them that they are going to pretend to be Drago again, fishing in the pool. Say *three* and let groups repeat it after you, while looking at the three crabs. (L1) Tell them to look at the bottom picture. Poor Drago! Say *four*, and the class repeats it in groups.

● Ask for volunteers to come out and act out the whole story: one child can be Drago and four children can be the crabs.

A–Z
● Point to the card with 4 on it and say *four*. Emphasize the initial sound /f/ and write 'f' on the board. Let the children pronounce the sound after you. Write the numeral '2' on the board. Point to it and say *two*. Emphasize the initial sound /t/ and write 't' on the board. Point to each letter and say the sound. Let the children repeat them after you.

● (L1) Tell the class that you are going to say one of the sounds and that you want someone to come up and point to the right letter. Do this a few times with different children, but only the ones who volunteer.

● Show the class the letter cards with 'f' and 't' on them. (L1) Ask volunteers to come up and match the cards to the right letters on the board. When they come up ask them if they can say the sound as well, but do not force them.

● (L1) Finally tell the children that you are going to trace in the air either 'f' or 't' and they have to identify which one it is, and say the sound. Trace the letter with your back to them. Do this a few times.

PB page 16
Ex. 1
● (L1) Explain to the class that they have to count the different objects on the page and draw a line to the correct numeral. Do the first example with the whole class. Show them how Tubs has drawn a line from the umbrella to number 1. Go around while the children are doing this and help them individually to count the objects. They can colour in the objects at the end.

Song
● Let the class listen to the song that they will learn in the next lesson.

LESSON 3

New language	Known language	
	one	three
	two	four

Preparation
● Write the numbers 1, 2, 3 and 4 several times on the board.

Revision
● (L1) Explain to the children that they have to join up the numbers on the board in the correct order, beginning with 1. Do one example with them. Ask for some children to come out and join 1 to 2, 2 to 3, etc. Make sure that every child that wants to has a turn.

PB page 17
Ex. 2
● (L1) Explain to the children that they have just joined up the numbers in the right order on the board. Now they have to do the same with Drago. Draw the

shape on the board first. Trace it in the air with your back to the class.

Let the children copy you using their forefinger. (L1) Tell them to trace over the dotted lines with their forefinger first beginning with his nose. Now let them use their pencils to join up the dots. Check that they are sitting properly. Go around and help those children who have difficulties.

PB page 17
Ex. 3

- (L1) Explain to the children that they are going to learn how to write the numbers. Follow the steps as for writing in the Introduction to the Teacher's Guide. (See page 6). First write '1' on the board. Next, with your back to the class, trace '1' in the air. Let them copy you, using their forefinger. They can trace it on their desk, on their friend's back, etc. (L1) Tell them to sit properly and trace over the numeral '1' with their forefinger. Now they can take their pencils, holding them correctly, and join the dots together. They can copy the number freehand underneath. Follow the same procedure with the other numbers.

Song

- Play the song and join in the words and do the actions. The children can sit and listen. The song is repeated on the cassette with pauses for the children to do the actions. Encourage them to join in the words when the song is repeated again on the cassette. Play the song right through again.

  Hop, one, two,
  Jump, three, four,
  Turn around quickly,
  And sit upon the floor.
  Clap, one, two,
  Knock, three, four,
  Jump up again,
  And be ready for more.

Further suggestions

- You may like to use the Ladybird number frieze to teach the numbers. Games to consolidate numbers can be played from *Bonanza*, e.g. 'How many teeth, Mr, Bear?' using the first four numbers only. Recommended books are: *I can count* (Ladybird); *Learn to count* (Ladybird).

Way in A: **Unit 5**

New language	Known language
a boat	That's a . . .
a fire	

Preparation
- Draw a boat at one end of the board and a fire at the other.
- Have three letter cards prepared, f, b, o.
- Make four flashcards: plane, boat, fire, fish.

Presentation
- Teach the new words. Point to the picture of the boat on the board and say *a boat*. Say it a few times and let the class repeat it. Divide the class into groups to repeat it. Do the same with *a fire*.
- (L1) Play 'Jumping the line'. Find an open area in the classroom. Draw a line in chalk on the floor and tell the class that one side is 'true' and the other 'false'. Explain that you are going to point to one of the pictures on the board and say either *boat* or *fire*. If you say *boat* and it is a boat then they jump to the true side. If you say *fire* when you are pointing to the boat then they jump to the false side. If a child makes a mistake then he or she is out. The game ends when all the players except one are out.

PB page 18
- Belinda and Tubs are on the beach. A boat comes into view. Belinda sees smoke and thinks that the boat is on fire. Tell the class to look at the top picture. Say *That's a boat*. Say it again and let the children repeat it after you. (L1) Tell them to look at the bottom picture. Say *That's a fire*. Repeat it and let the children repeat it after you. (L1) Check that the children understand what is happening in the story.

Practice
- Divide the class into two groups. Group A is Belinda and puts the Belinda puppet on, and group B is Tubs and puts the Tubs puppet on. Say *That's a boat*, and let group B say the sentence. Make sure they are looking at the boat. Say *That's a fire*. Group A repeats it after you. Change the groups around, and let them repeat the sentence. Divide the class into their usual groups to repeat each sentence.
- (L1) Ask if any of the children want to come out and act the story, using their puppets.

A–Z
- First revise 'f' and 'b'. Say *fire* and emphasize the initial letter /f/. Write 'f' on the board. Say the sound again and let the children repeat it after you. Do the same with *boat* and 'b'. Then point to each letter and say the sound. The children repeat it.
- (L1) Ask the class if they know what kind of animal Otto is. Tell them that he is an octopus. Say *octopus* and they repeat it. Emphasize the initial sound /o/. Write 'o' on the board. Teach the letter following the usual steps.
- Point to each letter and pronounce it. Let the children repeat each one after you. Show them the three letter cards and explain that you want three of them to come up and match the cards to the letters on the board. Do this a few times with different children.

Activity
- (L1) Explain that you are going to play a game. Sit the children in rows. Tell a child (Player 1) to walk up and down the rows and to stop behind any child. Explain that then you will show a letter card. Then the two children (Player 1 and the child sitting down) have to shout out the sound of the letter on the card. If Player 1 shouts out first and is right, then the child sitting down is out. If the other child shouts first and is right, then Player 1 is out and is replaced by the other child. Play it using the three letter cards only at first. You can then include the other letters that they have learnt.

LESSON 2

New language	Known language
a fish	That's a . . .
an elephant	

Preparation
- Draw a fish and an elephant on the board.

Presentation
- First teach the new language. Point to the picture of a fish on the board and say *fish* several times. Let the children repeat it after you. Then point to the picture of an elephant, and say *elephant*. Let the children repeat this after you. Say either *elephant* or *fish* and the children point to the correct picture.

PB page 19
- Drago and Otto are in the boat fishing. Drago is cooking a fish with his flames. Belinda arrives to put out the fire but upsets the boat.

- Tell the children to look at the top picture. Say *That's a fish*. Let the children repeat this after you. Then when they are looking at the bottom picture say *That's an elephant*. They repeat it. Do this several times.

Practice
- Divide the class into two groups. Group A is Otto; B is Drago. Say *That's a fish*. Group A repeats it. Remind them to look at the picture. Pretend to be Drago and say *That's an elephant*. Group B repeats it. Change the groups around. Divide the class into their usual smaller groups. Say each sentence and let group 1 repeat it after you, then group 2, and so on.

- (L1) Ask if four children would like to come out and act out the whole story.

Activities
- Draw a plane, a fish, a fire, a boat on the board and label them. Point to each picture and say the word. Let the children repeat it after you. (L1) Explain that you are going to say a word and one of them can come and point to the right word/ picture on the board.

- Show the class the flashcards one at a time and say the word. Let the class repeat them after you. (L1) Now ask for volunteers to come out and match the flashcards to the pictures/words on the board.

PB page 20 Ex. 1
- (L1) Explain to the class that they have to find the missing part of the picture and draw a line to the place where the part fits the picture. It's a jigsaw puzzle. Do the first example with the class. Go around and check their work.

PB page 20
Ex. 2

- Let the children shake their fingers on both hands to loosen them up. They must look at the board while you draw a ⌣ shape and a ⌐ shape. Next, with your back to the class trace 'j' in the air. Let the children copy you using their forefingers. Then they can trace it on their desks, on their friends' backs, etc. Do the same with the 'f' shape. Tell them to sit properly and place their books in front of them. Now they can trace over the dotted lines of the umbrella handles that Otto is holding with their forefinger and then join the dots with their pencils. Then the children can draw the three umbrella handles which are missing and colour in the picture.

Song

- If there is time play the song that they will learn next lesson.

LESSON 3

New language	Known language	
	a boat	a plane
	a bird	a fish

Preparation

- Draw pictures on the board of the following: a boat, a bird, a plane, a fish, and label them.

- Bring letter cards of all the letters taught: f, t, o, y, b, r, g.

- Prepare small plain pieces of paper, 4 for each group, to cover the letters on page 21.

Revision

- Divide the class into two teams, A and B. (L1) Explain that you are going to say one of the words that is on the board and when you do one child from each team must run out and point to the correct picture. The first child to point to the right picture wins a point for his or her team. Do this several times so that every child has a turn.

PB page 21
Ex. 3

- (L1) Explain to the class that they must listen to you very carefully and draw what you say in their books. Do the first one with the class as a whole.

  1) Draw a boat.
  2) Draw a bird.
  3) Draw a fish.
  4) Draw a plane.
  5) Draw an octopus.

  Say each one several times and give the children plenty of time to remember what the word is and draw it. Go over the activity with the class at the end.

PB page 21
Ex. 4

- Hold up the Belinda puppet and ask what it is. Say *elephant* and stress the initial sound /e/. Write 'e' on the blackboard. Let the children say it after you.

- (L1) Explain to the children that they are going to play a game, Letter Bingo, in groups. Divide the class into four groups and let each group choose which card they want to play with – Otto's card or Drago's, etc. Give each group four small pieces of paper. (L1) Explain that you are going to pick letters out of the bag and that you will say the sound and show them the letter and they must see if it is on their card. If it is, then they must put up their hand and say the sound. Then they must put a small piece of paper over the letter to cover it. The first group to have all their letters covered, shout BINGO! They have won. Play the game once so that they can see how it works. You can then change the cards around so that they play with different letters. You can play the game later in the course with other letters.

Song
● Now play the song for the children to listen to. (L1) Explain to them that it is about Drago and the boat. They can mime pouring on water at the appropriate time. When the song is repeated on the cassette join in the words and let the children clap to it. The third time they can join in the words.

> Drago's burning.
> Drago's burning.
> Get Belinda.
> Get Belinda.
> Fire, fire!
> Fire, fire!
> Pour on water.
> Pour on water.

Way in A: **Unit 6**

LESSON 1

New language	Known language
a nose	
an ear	
a head	
an eye	

Preparation
- Make letter cards for 'n' and 'h'.

Presentation
- Point to your nose and say *a nose*. Repeat this a few times. Gesture to the children to touch their noses and repeat *a nose* after you. Do the same with your ear. Say *an ear* and hold it.

- (L1) Explain that you are going to say one of these words and they must point to either their nose or their ear immediately otherwise they are out. After playing this several times teach *head* and *eye* in the same way. Now play the game using all four parts of the body.

- (L1) Ask the children what playground games they play. Do they play 'tag', where you have to chase and touch someone and then they are 'it'? The person who is 'it' then chases someone else and so on.

PB page 22
- Drago is trying to run past Otto without Otto touching him. But Otto touches Drago's nose. Drago now has to hold onto his nose until he touches someone else. Go through all the pictures and check that the children understand the story.
  (L1) Ask the children to look at the top picture. Say *a nose* and let the children repeat it. Do the same with *an ear* and *a head* in the other pictures.

Practice
- Divide the class up into their usual groups. Explain that Otto is saying *a nose*. Touch your nose and say *a nose* and let group 1 repeat it after you, then group 2 and so on. Do the same with the other items: ear, head. The children can put on a puppet of their choice in order to touch their nose, ear and head. This will make it more exciting for them.

- (L1) Finally ask if any of the children want to come out and act the story.

A–Z
- Explain to the children that they are going to learn two more letters. Say *nose* and emphasize the initial sound /n/. Write 'n' on the board. Say *head*, emphasize the initial sound /h/ and write 'h' on the board. Point to the two sounds and say them again. Let the children repeat them after you. Do this several times. Make sure that you are always pointing to the right letter and that the children are looking at the one that they are pronouncing.

- Tell the children that you are going to say one of the sounds and you want one of them to come up and point to the right letter. Do this several times.

- Now show the class the two letter cards with 'h' and 'n' on them. Tell the children that you want two of them to come up and match the cards to the right letters on the board. When they come up ask them if they can say the sound as well.

- Write five other letters they have learnt on the board too – g, y, b, o and k. Point to each one and say the sound. Let the children repeat it after you. Tell them to look at the board and try to remember what the letters are. They can have one minute to look and memorize them. After one minute tell them to close their eyes and not to look at what you are doing. Rub off one letter. They can then open their eyes and put up their hands if they know the letter that has gone and they can say the sound. You may play this a few times.

Activity
- You may like to go outside and play 'tag' just like the characters in the book. Go over the rules again with the class. (L1) Tell them that they can only touch the other person on the nose, the head, the ear. Let's leave the eye out! When the child who is 'it' touches somebody he or she must name the part of the body touched in English or the child has not been 'tagged'. Play this for a short time only. You can always play it again in another lesson.

LESSON 2

New language	Known language
a leg	an elephant
a tail	

Preparation
- Draw a nose, head, eye, and ear, on the left side of the board and a duplicate set on the right and label them.
- Have ready your Belinda puppet.

Revision
- Quickly play the game from the previous lesson where you say *a nose* and the children have to point to the right part of the body as quickly as possible, otherwise they are out.

Presentation
- Quickly draw a tail on the board. Point to it and say *a tail*. Let the children say this after you a few times. Next point to your leg and say *a leg*. Say it several times and let the children repeat it after you. Hold up Belinda and ask what animal she is. The children say *an elephant*.

PB page 23
- Tell the class to look at the top picture. Drago has seen something sticking out of a bush. Pretend to be Drago. Look puzzled and say *What's this? A tail*. Look at the middle picture. Drago pulls at the tail and discovers it is attached to a leg. Say *A leg*. Now look at the bottom picture. Drago has pulled hard and found Belinda was the owner of the leg and tail. Laugh and say *An elephant!*

Practice
- (L1) Now ask if three children can come out and act the story. Tell one child to hide under the desk and tie a piece of string on him or her to represent the tail. Explain that they must do the actions as they are in the story. You and the class together then say *What's this?* The child playing Drago sniffs at the tail and 'Tubs' looks surprised. All together you say *A tail!* Then Drago pulls at the string and pretends to bite Belinda's leg. Everyone says *A leg!* Tubs then goes over and looks closely at it.

Then Belinda is pulled out by Drago and looks angry. Everyone says *An elephant!* If there is time perhaps three more children would like to come out and act the parts. Encourage them to say the words as they do so.

Activities

- Point to the four pictures on the board in turn and say the words. Point silently and encourage the class to tell you what they are. Go over them again pointing to the words underneath and saying *nose*, etc. The class look at the words and repeat them after you. Do the same with the other words.

- Point to the duplicate pictures and words on the board. Ask if some children would like to come out and point to two pictures which match. After doing this several times then rub out the pictures on the left side and ask the children to match the word on the left to the picture plus word on the right.

PB page 24 Ex. 1

- (L1) Explain to the children that they have to draw a line from the word to the picture. Do the first example with the class. Go around and help those who need it. Remember to praise and encourage them.

PB page 24 Ex. 2

- Explain to the class they are going to join the dots from left to right. What will it make? – the sea. Show them first on the board how to join up the pattern – an up and a down movement. With your back to them, show them how to do the pattern using their forefinger. Let them loosen up their hands and fingers first by shaking them. They can trace the movement in the air, on their friends' backs, on their desks. Show them how to hold the pencil and remind them to sit properly. Let them trace over the pattern in their books with their forefinger first and then join up the dots. They must get a flowing action. When they have finished they can colour in the picture.

Rhyme

- If there is time at the end of the lesson, you can play the class the rhyme that they are to learn next lesson.

LESSON 3

New language	Known language	
a hand	a nose	an ear
	a leg	a head
	an eye	

Preparation

- Draw the parts of the body on the board and label them: hand, tail, nose, leg, ear, eye, head. Separately write the words again at the other end of the board.

Revision

- Point to the different parts of your body and say *What's this?* The class answers. Next say the names and they have to touch those parts of their body as quickly as possible.

Presentation

- Hold up your hand and say *a hand* several times. The children hold up their hands and repeat *a hand* a few times.

● (L1) Explain to the children that you are going to name a part of the body and one of them has to come and point to it on the board. Do this with all the items. Point to the words that have been written separately on the board. (L1) Explain to the children that they have to come up and join the word 'nose' to the picture/word of a nose. Ask for volunteers and do this with all the items. Next rub out the words underneath the pictures and encourage the children to come up and join the isolated words to the pictures. If they find this difficult do not force them.

PB page 25
Ex. 3

● (L1) Explain to the children that in order to finish this picture they have to join all the dots together. First though they have to listen to you. (L1) Tell them that you will say a word e.g. *hand* and they have to find it on the picture and join the dots. Do the first one with the whole class. Say *leg*. Go around and make sure that the children are joining up the right dots. Now do the rest of the exercise: *1) eye   2) ear   3) nose   4) hand   5) head.*
Say the word several times for them to find it and join up the dots. When they have finished go around and check that they know the words for the parts of the body. Say *What's this?* and point to a part of the body. When they are finished ask them what the picture is of. Say he is a *clown*. Then let them colour the clown.

Rhyme

● Tell the class that you are going to teach them a new rhyme. They must listen to it and watch your actions. Play the rhyme and when the different parts of the body are mentioned, touch them. When you come to 'And now fly!' you should flap your arms as if trying to fly. Play the rhyme again, join in the words yourself and ask the children to clap and do the actions. Finally, encourage them to join in with the words and actions.

1   Touch your head,
    Touch your nose,
    Touch your tail,
    Touch your toes.

2   Touch your leg,
    Touch your eye,
    Touch your ear,
    And now fly!

Way in A: **Unit 7**

LESSON 1

New language	Known language
I have a . . .	
a book	
a mouse	
an apple	

Preparation
- Draw a book, a mouse and an apple on the board and label them.

Presentation
- Hold up a book and say *a book*. Say this a few times. Let the children hold up their books and say *a book*. Ask group 1 to say *a book*, then group 2 and so on. Point to the mouse on the board and say *a mouse*. Let the children repeat it a few times. Each group can repeat it.

- (L1) Explain that you will say either *a book* or *a mouse* and they must either hold up the book or point to the picture, whichever is correct.

- Now put your book under your arm and say *I have a book*. (L1) Check that the children understand the meaning. Say it a few times. Let the class hold their books and say *I have a book*. They repeat it in their groups.

PB page 26
- Belinda has received a parcel. It's a book. Drago is hiding behind a tree and decides to play a joke on her with a mouse. (L1) Check that the children understand the situation. Tell them to look at the top picture. Say *I have a book*. The class repeats it. They look at the bottom picture. Say *I have a mouse*. Let them repeat it after you a few times.

Practice
- Divide the class up into two groups only at first. (L1) Remind them to look at the pictures and tell them that group A is going to be Belinda and group B Drago. They put on the appropriate puppets. Say *I have a book*. Group A repeats it after you. Say *I have a mouse*. Group B repeats it. Change the groups around and do it again.

- Divide the class up into their usual smaller groups. Pretend to be Belinda and say *I have a book*. Group 1 repeats it after you, group 2, etc. Pretend to be Drago and say *I have a mouse*. Each group repeats it after you, wearing the appropriate puppets.

- (L1) Ask if any two children would like to come out and act the story. One could be the cat, and one the mouse.

A–Z
- Point to the mouse on the board and say *mouse*. Emphasize the initial sound /m/ and write 'm' on the board. Point to it, pronounce the sound and let the children say it after you. Point to the apple and say *apple*. Emphasize the initial sound /a/ and write 'a' on the board. Pronounce the sound and let the class repeat it.

Activity
- Play 'Drago says . . .'. (L1) Explain to the class that you are going to give orders and they must obey them, but only if the orders are introduced by the phrase, *Drago says* . . . . If they do not obey the orders then they are out. Make sure the class understands the orders first. Use *Touch your* . . . and include objects and parts of the

body that the children know. Begin the game. Teacher: *Drago says, 'Touch your book'*. (The children touch their books.) *Touch your leg*. Any child who touches his or her leg is out as you did not say *Drago says . . . .* The child left at the end is the winner.

LESSON 2	New language	Known language
	a cat	I have a . . .
		an apple

Preparation
- Draw a picture of a cat, an octopus and an apple on the board and label them.

- Make three letter cards: 'c', 'o', 'a'.

Presentation
- Point to the picture of a cat and say *a cat* several times and the children repeat it after you. Point to the apple and say *an apple* a few times and the children repeat it.

PB page 27
- Belinda is frightened by the mouse but she has a cat and the cat chases the mouse away. Drago is angry that his joke hasn't worked out. (L1) Check that the children understand the situation. When looking at the second picture pretend to be Belinda and say *I have a cat*. The class repeat it after you.

Practice
- Divide the class up into groups. Everyone puts on the Belinda puppet and pretends to be Belinda. Say *I have a cat*. Each group repeats it after you in turn.

- Encourage the children to come out and act out the whole story. One child is Drago, one Belinda, one the cat and another the mouse.

A–Z
- Point to the picture of the cat and let the children say *cat*. You say it and emphasize the initial sound /k/. Write 'c' on the board. Say it again and let the children repeat it. Point to the octopus and say *octopus*. The children repeat it. Say it and emphasize the initial sound /o/. Write 'o' on the board. Say it again and let the children repeat it after you. Point to the apple and let the class say *apple*. Say it and emphasize the initial sound /a/. Write 'a' on the board. Say the sound again and let the children say it after you.

- Give the three letter cards 'o', 'a' and 'c' to volunteers. They come up and match the cards to the letters on the blackboard.

PB page 28 Ex. 1
- (L1) Explain to the class that they are going to learn how to form the letters 'o', 'a' and 'c'. First draw large circles on the board in an anti-clockwise direction. Then trace them in the air with your back to the children and let them copy you. They can trace the circles in the air, on their desks, etc. Then let the children trace over the circles at the top of the page with their forefingers. The children can then join the dots with their pencils.

- Next they must trace over the four 'o's in their books with their forefingers. They then join the dots underneath and finally write the 'o's freehand on the line. They can fill in the 'o's in octopus.

- Do the same with 'c' and 'a'.

Song
- Let the class listen to the song that they will learn next lesson.

LESSON 3

New language	Known language	
an apple	a mouse	
a cat	a book	

Preparation
- Draw an apple, a cat, a mouse, a book on the board and label them, one in each corner of the board.

- Make flashcards for these words: cat, mouse, book, apple.

PB page 29
Ex. 2
- The friends have got their pieces of string tangled up. The children have to help untangle them. (L1) Tell them to take a coloured pencil and follow Belinda's string to find what she has. Then they can take a different colour and follow Otto's. They can use a different coloured pencil for each character. When they have completed this task they can see which animal has which object. (L1) Explain that they are now going to be the characters and say what they have. Belinda says *I have a cat*; Drago says *I have a mouse*; Otto says *I have a book*; and Tubs says *I have an apple*.

Activities
- Hold up a book. Let the children tell you it's *a book*. You say, *a book*. Now hold up the flashcard and say *book*. Let the children look and repeat it. Do this several times. Point to the picture of a cat and let the children say *a cat*. Hold up the flashcard and say *cat*. The children look and repeat it.

- (L1) Ask if some volunteers can come out and match the cards to the words. Then show the class the flashcards. If it is 'book' they look at it and hold up a book. If it is 'cat' then they point to the picture on the board. Do this silently.

- Teach them 'apple' and 'mouse' in the same way.

- Put the four cards on the floor and ask if there is any child who can jump from one to the other and say the words correctly. If they can't they'll fall in the river and get eaten by a hungry crocodile!

Song
- Play the song 'I have a house' for the class to learn. Play it and join in the words while the class listen and clap. Play it again and encourage them to join in with the words.

1 I have a house
And in my house,
I have a floor
And a window and a door.

2 I have a house,
And in my house,
I have a cat
And a rabbit and a hat.

Way in A: **Unit 8**

LESSON 1

New language	Known language
five	one
six	two
an egg	three
a zebra	four

Preparation
- Bring in six stones and a ball.
- On the board draw the numerals 1–6 on one side and 'dominoes' 1–6 on the other.
- Draw an egg on the board.
- Make letter cards for 'e', 's' and 'd'.

Revision
- (L1) Tell the children that you have a number of stones in your hand and that they have to guess how many there are. Use only four stones at the moment. They guess *two* or *four*, etc.
- Then tell them that you are going to knock on the desk and they have to tell you how many times you have knocked.

Presentation
- (L1) Check that the children are familiar with the numbers in their mother tongue up to 8. Hold up five fingers and count *one, two, three, four, five*. Repeat *five* and hold up five fingers. Let the children imitate you; they repeat the sequence and hold up their fingers. Count from 1 to 5 with them again. (If you have a number frieze you may like to use that.) Write 5 ⚅ on the board. Teach *six* in the same way. Write 6 ⚅ on the board.
- Play a numbers game with the children. Explain to them that you are going to say a number and then they must clap the right number of times. For example you say *five* and they must clap five times. Play this with all the numbers from 1–5.

PB page 30
- Belinda and Tubs are collecting lemons. (L1) Tell the class to put on the Belinda or Tubs puppet and say that you are all going to count the lemons together. (L1) Now tell the class to look at the top of the page. Look at the number and at the number of dots. Tell them to count the dots aloud.

Practice
- Divide the class into their groups. Count the lemons, *one, two, three, four, five*. Group 1 counts them after you, then group 2, and so on. Count the lemons at the bottom. Say *one, two, three, four, five, six*. Each group counts them after you.

A–Z
- Point to the picture of the egg on the board and say *egg*, emphasizing the initial sound /e/. Write 'e' on the board. Say the sound and let the children repeat it after you. Write '6' on the board and say *six*. Emphasize the initial sound /s/ and write 's'. Point to the door and say *door*. Emphasize the initial sound /d/ and write 'd' on the board. Finally point to each letter and say its sound and let the children repeat them after you.

- Give out the three letter cards to volunteers and ask them to match the card to the letter on the board. Do this a few times with different children.

Activities
- Take the children outside for this game. Give each child a number from 1–6. (L1) Explain that you are going to throw up the ball and call out a number. If the number is theirs then they have to run and catch the ball before it bounces, and before the other children with the same number get to it.

- Point to the numbers on the board and say *one* when pointing to 1, etc. Point to the 'dominoes' and say the numbers. (L1) Explain to the children that they can come up individually and join the right number to the right 'domino'. Give every child the opportunity to come out but do not force them. Encourage them to say the number.

Further suggestions
- You may like to play more numbers games. *Bonanza* has several of them: 'How many Teeth, Mr Bear?' 'Groups of Five.' 'Giant Steps and Fairy Steps.'

LESSON 2

New language	Known language
seven	one–six
eight	a zebra

Preparation
- Bring in eight stones.

Revision
- Write the numbers 1–6 all over the board. Make sure that the children can reach them. Point to each number in order and say *one*, *two*, etc. and let the class repeat them after you. Now you point at random and they say the number.

- Divide the class into two teams, A and B. Explain that you are going to call out a number and the first child from each team should run out and put a ring around the number. The first to do it gets a point for his or her team. Call out numbers at random.

Presentation
- Check that the children are familiar with the concepts of seven and eight in their mother tongue. Hold up seven fingers and count from one to seven, (or use a number frieze). Let the children count with you using their fingers. Do it again. Write

  7 [:::] on the left of the board and say *seven*. Let the children repeat this after you. Teach 'eight' in the same way. Write 8 [::::] on the right of the board.

- (L1) Explain to the children that you are going to say a number, either 7 or 8, and they have to point to the right one on the board. Do this a few times.

PB page 31
- Belinda and Tubs are collecting even more lemons. One is going to fall on Belinda's head! (L1) Tell the children to count the lemons in the top picture, and then in the bottom picture. Ask them to look at the top picture again. Count the lemons. The children count after you. Then they can look at the bottom picture. You count to eight and the class counts after you.

Practice	• Divide the class into groups. (L1) Ask them to put on their Tubs or Belinda puppet and count the lemons in the top picture and then in the bottom picture. Count with them, group 1 first, then group 2, and so on.
	• (L1) Ask if three children want to come out and mime or act the story.
Activity	• Divide the class quickly into two teams, A and B. Tell them that you are going to say a number and team A has to clap the correct number of times. If they are right then they get a point. Do the same for team B. Cover all the numbers 1–8 in this way.
PB page 32 Ex. 1	• (L1) Ask the children what Otto is doing. With your back to the class make flowing movements in the air. Tell them to copy you, using their forefingers. Then let them trace the movements on their desks etc., again with their fingers. (L1) Explain that they have to join up the dots at the top of the page. First though let them trace over the dots with their fingers, then they can use their pencils to join them up. Go around and make sure that they are joining the dots from left to right and from top to bottom.
	• Now draw an egg on the board and say *egg*, emphasizing the sound /e/. Let the children look and pronounce the sound after you. Trace the shape of the letter in the air with your back to the class and the children then copy you, using their forefingers. They can trace the shape on their friends' backs, etc. (L1) Tell them to trace over the word 'egg' in their books with their fingers. Then they can join up the dots with their pencils and finally write a line of 'e's and the word egg. Remind them to sit properly, have their books in front of them and hold their pencils between their thumb and forefinger. Go around and help each child, showing them how to form the letter on their page.
	• Teach 's' and 'd' in the same way.
Song	• If there is time let them sit quietly and listen to the song that you will teach them next lesson.

LESSON 3

New language	Known language
	one–eight

Preparation	• Bring in a soft bag.
	• Write 5, 6, 7 and 8 on the board and label them.
	• Make flashcards for five, six, seven, eight.
Revision	• Take the children outside. Divide the class into two teams. Line the teams up opposite one another. Give out the numbers 1–8 down the lines. Number 1 in team A faces number 1 in team B, etc. (If there are more than 16 children then you can have two games going simultaneously.) Put a chair half-way between the two teams. On the chair put an object, a bag perhaps, (something that can be picked up without

tearing). (L1) Explain that you are going to call out a number, e.g. '7'. The children who have that number, from both teams, run to the centre. They try to get the object, and then run back to their place without being touched by the other '7'. If they are not touched then they score a point for their team. The object is then returned to the chair. Everyone has a turn. The team with the most points is the winner.

PB page 33 Ex. 2
- (L1) Tell the children that they have to count the number of circles, stars, etc. and write in the correct number. Go over the first one, the circles, with them. Tell them to be careful with the last one. Many children will think that there are only four squares. Make sure that they understand that the answer is five (four little squares inside a fifth big square).

PB page 33 Ex. 3
- Before you begin the exercise point to the numbers on the board and let the children say what they are. Point to '5' and say *five*. The children repeat it. Hold up the flashcard and say *five*. The class look and repeat it. Do the same with '6', '7' and '8'. Ask for four volunteers to match the flashcards to the numerals/words.

- (L1) Explain that in the bottom exercise the children have to count the books, eyes, etc. Then they have to join the picture to the right number in the boxes on Tubs' back. Do the first example, the five books, with the whole class. They can join up the dots that form the word at the end.

Song
- Play the song 'One, two' and do the actions while the children watch and listen. Then sing the first two lines, do the actions, and tell the children to do the actions with you. (Be careful with 'Run to the door', otherwise you may have a stampede!) Go through the whole song in this way.

One, two,
Touch your shoe.
Three, four,
Run to the door.
Five, six,
Pick up sticks.
Seven, eight,
Open the gate.

Way in A: **Unit 9**

LESSON 1

New language	Known language
a T.V.	What's this?
a radio	

Preparation
- Draw a plane, a boat, a T.V. and a radio on the board. Label them.
- Make letter cards for 'b', 'h' and 'p'.

Presentation
- Teach the new words. Point to the picture of the T.V. on the board and say *a T.V.* Let the children repeat this after you. Say it several times and let the children repeat it. Do the same with the picture of the radio.

PB page 34
- Drago is puzzled by what he's found. He investigates the T.V. and then the radio. Drago eats the radio! Tell the class to look at the top picture. Say *a T.V.* They repeat this. Say *a radio* and remind the children to look at the radio when they say it.

Practice
- Divide the class up into their groups. They are all going to put on their Drago puppet and pretend to be Drago. Say *a T.V.* and group 1 repeats this, then group 2, and so on. Say *a radio* and group 2 repeats this, then group 3, and so on finishing with group 1.
- (L1) Ask if a child would like to come out and mime being Drago.

A–Z
- Point to the picture of the plane on the board and say *What's this?* The children say *a plane.* You repeat it and emphasize the initial sound /p/. Write 'p' on the board. Point to your head and ask *What's this?* Wait until the children say *a head.* Repeat *head* and emphasize the initial sound /h/ and write 'h' on the board. Point to the picture of the boat and ask *What's this?* When the children say *boat* repeat *boat* and emphasize the initial sound /b/. Then write 'b' on the board. Point to the three letters and say each sound and the class repeats them after you. Make sure that the children are looking at the letter when they are saying the sound.
- Give out the three letter cards, 'b', 'p', and 'h' and let the children come out and match the cards to the letters on the board.
- Then tell the children that you are going to say a sound and one of them can come up and put a ring around the correct letter. Do this several times to give each child the opportunity to have a turn. Encourage the children to say the sound as they ring the letter.

Activity
- Draw an incomplete picture on the board. It can be any object that the children know the name for in English, e.g. ladder, kite. Say *What's this?* The children have to guess. The first one to guess can come up and draw an incomplete picture on the board and say *What's this?* Continue with the game so that the majority of the children have a turn.

LESSON 2	New language	Known language
		What's this?
		a radio

PB page 35
- Drago has a stomach ache. He is very sick. Belinda and Tubs are worried. Belinda listens to Drago's stomach and wonders what it is. Tubs knows – Drago has eaten a radio! Let them look at the top picture. Say *What's this?* Say it a few times and let the children repeat it after you. They look at the bottom picture. Say *A radio*. Say it a few times and let the children repeat it.

Practice
- Divide the class into their groups. Tell them to use the Drago and Belinda puppets. First of all you demonstrate. Hold up the Belinda puppet and put her trunk next to Drago's stomach and say *What's this?* Let group 1 repeat this after you, then group 2 and so on, Now, using the Tubs and Drago puppets, hold up Tubs and say *a radio* while he is sitting on Drago's stomach. Let group 1 repeat it after you, and so on.

- (L1) Ask if any three children would like to come out and act or mime the whole story.

**PB page 36
Ex. 1**
- What is happening to Belinda? Encourage the class to tell you. Ask the children to join the dotted lines in the fence, from top to bottom. This will give them practice in downward strokes.

- Now demonstrate how to form 'b'. Let the children trace it in the air, on the page and then join the dots with their pencils. Finally they can write the letter freehand and form the word. The shape on the right can be coloured in using a blue crayon.

- Teach 'h' and 'p' in the same way.

Song
- If there is time at the end let the class listen to the song that they will learn in the next lesson.

LESSON 3	New language	Known language
	one–eight	a T.V.
	a cat	a radio
	a mouse	

Preparation
- Draw pictures on the board of a cat, a mouse, a T.V. and a radio. Write the words underneath. Draw a duplicate set on the other side of the board.

Revision
- Write the numbers 1–8 on the board at random. Ask a child to come up and join 1 to 2. Then another one can come up and join 2 to 3 and so on. This is to check that they know the sequence of numbers.

PB page 37
Ex. 2

- (L1) Explain to the children that they have to join up the dots in the right order and then decide what the picture is. Underneath they have to write its name. Go around and help the children who have difficulties. When everyone has finished say *What's this?* and the children answer, *A plane.*

Activity

- Explain to the class that you want them to look at the board. Tell them that you want one of them to come out and pick a picture/word and then match it with the equivalent picture/word from the other side of the board. When children come up encourage them to say the name of the object they point to.

- Now rub out the pictures in one set, leaving the words only. Ask them to join the correct word to the word/picture. Again encourage each child that comes up to say the name.

- Finally rub out the words that are underneath the pictures so that the children have to match the picture to the right word. Ask for volunteers. If they are unable to do this at this point do not push them.

PB page 37
Ex. 3

- (L1) Explain that the children have to join up the dots around the picture and the dotted words next to the pictures and then match these to the printed words. Do 'T.V.' with them first. Go around and check their work.

Song

- Play the song on the cassette. Let the children listen to it while you join in with the words. Play it again and let the children clap to it. When the parts of the body are mentioned touch each one. Play it again and encourage the children to join in with the words.

  > I have ten little fingers
  > And ten little toes.
  > I have ten little fingers
  > And ten little toes.
  > I have two ears,
  > I have two eyes,
  > And just one little nose.

Way in A: **Unit 10**

New language	Known language
It's . . .	red
black	yellow
white	blue
grey	green
brown	

Preparation

● Bring some coloured chalk – white, brown and grey.

● Have ready brown, black, grey and white coloured cards, and flashcards with the names of the colours written on them.

● Have 4 small coloured strips of paper for each child – 1 for each of the new colours.

● Bring the other coloured cards, red, blue, yellow and green.

Revision

● Line up the coloured cards, red, blue, green, yellow at one end of the classroom. First point to each colour and say its name. Go to the other end of the room with the children. Divide them into two teams. (L1) Explain that you are going to say the name of the colour and one person from each team has to run to the cards and select the right colour. The first one to pick up the card is the winner.

Presentation

● (L1) Check that the children know the new colours, brown, black, white and grey, in their mother tongue. Hold up the black card and say *black*. Let the children repeat this. Say it several times and the children can repeat it in their groups. Now hold up the white card and say *white*. Let the children repeat this after you. Put the black card in one hand and the white card in the other. (L1) Explain to the children that you are going to say the name of either colour and they must point to the correct one. Do this several times.

● Now teach grey and brown in the same way.

PB page 38

● The friends are painting. Otto is painting Tubs' shell. Drago and Belinda are mixing their colours accidentally. (L1) Tell the children to look at Drago and say *It's black*. Let them repeat this after you several times. Then let them look at Belinda. Say *It's white*. Say this a few times and then the children repeat it after you. Next they look at the grey puddle made where the black and white paint has run together and say *It's grey*. Make sure that they are looking at the right colour when they say it. Look at Tubs now. Say *It's brown*. Say it several times and let the children repeat it.

Practice

● Divide the class into their groups. They are going to put each of the puppets on in turn and pretend to be the different characters. First of all, Drago: you say *It's black*. Group 1 repeats it, group 2, and so on. Then they are Belinda: you say *It's white*. Each group repeats it after you. Vary the order of the groups. Finally they pretend to be Otto and say *It's brown*.

● Ask if any four children would like to come out and act the story, pretending that they have tins of paint. They could use the coloured cards as the tins.

A–Z
- Quickly revise the letter shapes and sounds for 'r', 'n' and 'm'. Say *red* and emphasize the initial sound /r/ and write 'r' on the board. Say *nose* and emphasize the initial sound /n/ and write 'n' on the board. Say *mouse* and emphasize the initial sound /m/ and write 'm' on the board.

- (L1) Explain to the class that you are going to say two sounds and that they have to tell you whether they are the same or different.

  1) /m/ /m/; 2) /r/ /n/; 3) /n/ /n/; 4) /m/ /r/; 5) /r/ /r/.

Activity
- Write the words 'black', 'grey', 'white' and 'brown' on the board. Hold up each coloured card and wait for the children to tell you which it is. When they do, stick or hold the card underneath the name of the colour on the board, so that the black card is under the word 'black'. Let the children look at the card and the word and say *black*. Do this for all four words.

- Now give each child the four coloured strips of paper – brown, grey, white and black. (L1) Tell the class that you are going to say the name of one of the four new colours. They must then hold up the correct coloured strip. Do this several times with all the colours.

- (L1) Now explain to the children that you are going to hold up a flashcard with the name of one of the colours on it. They have to look at it and look at the board and then hold up the correct coloured strip again. If they find difficulty with this, say the name of the colour, too, when holding up the card.

LESSON 2

New language	Known language	
red	black	
yellow	green	
brown	white	
blue	grey	
It's . . .		

Preparation
- Bring in all the coloured cards.

Revision
- (L1) Explain to the children that you are going to hold up a coloured card and say its name. If it is right then they have to repeat it and if it is not then they must remain silent.

PB page 39
- Belinda is twirling the umbrella and where it stops each character has to say what colour it is: it's a game. (L1) Tell them to look at Drago. Say *It's yellow*. Let the children repeat it. Do the same with the other characters and colours.

Practice
- Divide the class up into their groups. Remind the class to look at the correct colours as they say them. Everyone is going to pretend to be the different characters in turn, using the puppets. Pretend to be Drago: say *It's yellow*. Group 1 to repeat it after you, group 2, and so on. Continue with the other characters.

- (L1) Ask if any of them would like to come out and mime or act the situation. If you have been able to bring in a coloured umbrella you can use it at this point. Twirl it around and the individual children say the colour it stops at.

**PB page 40
Ex. 1**

- First write the pattern on the board. (L1) Tell the class to look at what you are doing carefully. Trace the pattern in the air with your back to the class. What does it remind them of? (A parachute!) Let the children trace the pattern in their books with their fingers, then join the dots with a pencil. It will help in the formation of the letters they are about to learn.

- Point to something red and say *red.* Say the sound /r/ and write 'r' on the board. Tell the class, with their forefingers to trace it in the air. Then they can trace it on their desks, on their friends' backs, etc. Next tell them to trace over the letter on the page and finally join the dots together and write the word 'red'. They have to colour in the shape with a red pencil. Then they can form their 'r's underneath.

- Follow the same steps with 'n' and 'm'. Remind them to sit properly, put their books straight in front of them and hold their pencils correctly. Go around and help each child form some of the letters.

Song

- Play the song at the end of the lesson for the children to clap to and listen to before they learn it in the next lesson.

LESSON 3

New language	Known language	
	white	blue
	black	green
	brown	yellow
	grey	

Preparation

- Bring in the coloured cards.

- Bring 2 clothes pegs or adhesive tape.

Revision

- Take the children outside to play 'Dance of the ostriches'. Divide the class into two teams. Select one child from each team and stand them facing one another. Attach one coloured card to the back of each child. Tell the children to put their hands behind their backs. (L1) Explain to the children that they have to dance around each other and try to see what colour is on the other child's back. The first to do so is the winner and gains a point for the team. After these two have competed then it is the turn of the next two.

**PB page 41
Ex. 2**

- (L1) Explain to the children that they are going to colour Otto's pictures. You are going to tell them what colour to use. First ask them to tell you the names of the animals. They say *a cat, a bird, a mouse* and *an elephant.* Now give the instructions:

1) Colour the cat white.
2) Colour the bird black.
3) Colour the mouse brown.
4) Colour the elephant grey.

Say the instruction several times so that the children have the opportunity to get the exercise right. Now tell them to join up the dots underneath to form the words. Go around and help those children who have difficulties. Go over the whole task with the class.

PB page 41
Ex. 3

● (L1) First, hold up the blue card and give the class the opportunity to tell you what colour it is. Do the same with yellow and green. Second, hold up the flashcard with 'blue' on it and say *blue*. Let the class repeat it after you. Do the same with *green* and *yellow*. Stick the coloured cards with the three flashcards next to them on the board so that the children can refer to them for this exercise. (L1) Tell the children that they have to read the names of the colours and colour in the paint correctly. Go around and check that they are doing this. Help individual children.

Song

● Play the song for the children to listen to first while you sing along with it. Play it again and they can clap. Finally, encourage them to join in the words with you.

The hen is white,
The bird is black,
The fish is grey,
Now turn your back.
The cat is grey,
The mouse is brown,
The dog is white,
Now turn around.

Way in A: **Unit 11**

New language	Known language
I like . . .	yellow
cake	an umbrella
bread	
chocolate	

Preparation

- Bring in some cake, some chocolate and some bread or draw them on the board.

- Make letter cards for 'u' and 'y'.

Presentation

- Teach the new words. Hold up the chocolate and say *chocolate*. Let the children repeat it after you. Ask who likes chocolate. All those who do must repeat after you: *I like chocolate*. Teach *bread* and *cake* in the same way.

- Play 'Jumping the line'. Remind the children of the game. Draw a line. One side is 'true' and the other side is 'false'. If you hold up the bread and say *chocolate* then they jump to the 'false' side. If you hold up cake and say *cake* then they jump to the 'true' side. Play this until you are sure they know the words and their meanings.

PB page 42

- The friends are having a picnic. Belinda likes bread so she is eating a lot of it. Otto likes chocolate and he is getting it all over his face. Tubs likes cake so much he gets inside it! Do the children like picnics? Tell them to look at the top picture. Pretend to be Belinda and say *I like bread*. Do the same with Otto, *I like chocolate*. Then Tubs, *I like cake*.

Practice

- Divide the class up into groups. Pretend to be Belinda and say *I like bread*. Let group 1 repeat it after you, then group 2, and so on, using their Belinda puppets. Remind the class to look at the picture. Pretend to be Otto and say *I like chocolate*. Let group 1 repeat it after you, group 2, and so on. Pretend to be Tubs and say *I like cake*. Let group 1 repeat it after you, then group 2.

- (L1) Ask if three children would like to come out and act or mime the picnic. You can give them the food to hold.

A–Z

- Point to something yellow and say *yellow*. Emphasize the initial sound /j/ and write 'y' on the board. Draw an umbrella quickly on the board. Say *umbrella* and emphasize the initial sound /ʌ/. Write 'u' on the board. Point to each letter and say the sound. Let the class repeat it after you. Make sure that they are looking at the letter when you are pointing to it.

- Ask for two children to match the two letter cards with 'y' and 'u' on them to the letters on the board. Do this with several different children, but only ones who volunteer.

- (L1) Tell the class that you are going to trace one of the letters in the air with your back to them and they have to identify whether it is 'y' or 'u'. If they can do this easily include other letters that they have learnt.

Optional activity

- Give the children some paper. Tell them that they can draw on it what food they particularly like. They can then colour it and cut it out. You will probably have to help them with the cutting out. When they have finished you can either:
  i) stick all the pictures on a large piece of paper and make a collage.
  ii) stick thread or string on the drawings and make a mobile of them, or hang them around the classroom.
  The children could do the drawings for homework.

LESSON 2

New language	Known language
I don't like . . .	cake
ice cream	bread
	chocolate

Preparation

- Bring in some bread, some cake, some chocolate and a picture of some ice cream.

- Draw some chocolate, bread, cake, ice cream on the board and label them. Make flashcards for them.

Revision

- Lay out the food on the desk in front of the children and point to each item and say *bread, cake,* etc. Let the children repeat them after you. (L1) Explain that you are going to cover the food up with a cloth and they are going to close their eyes while you remove one of the items. They will open their eyes when you tell them to and then they must tell you in English which is missing. Do this a few times removing different objects each time. If you have only the pictures on the board rub one off instead.

Presentation

- Show the class the picture of the ice cream and say *ice cream.* Ask them to repeat it after you. Say it a few times and they can repeat it in their groups. Now lick your lips and say *I like ice cream.* They all repeat this after you. Say it several times and they can repeat it in their different groups. (L1) Ask the class if there is anyone who *doesn't* like ice cream. Tell them that you don't. Make a grimace and say: *I don't like ice cream.* Say it a few times. (L1) Explain that now they have to pretend that they don't like ice cream so they can repeat after you: *I don't like ice cream.* They repeat this several times.

PB page 43

- Drago is trying to eat the ice cream but every time he has a lick flames come out and it melts! Tubs is licking up Drago's ice cream. He likes it. (L1) Tell the children to look at Drago. Say *I don't like ice cream.* Say it a few times and the children can repeat it. (L1) Tell them to look at Tubs. Say *I like ice cream.* Say it a few times and let the class repeat it.

Practice

- Divide the class up into their groups. Tell them to pretend to be Drago and Tubs. Be Drago first. Say *I don't like ice cream.* Group 1 repeats it, then group 2, and so on. Pretend to be Tubs and say, *I like ice cream.* Group 1 repeats it, then group 2, and so on.

- (L1) Ask if any of them would like to come out and act the situation.

- (L1) Now ask who truthfully likes ice cream and who doesn't. Tell those who like ice cream to say they do. They say *I like ice cream*. (L1) Tell those that don't like ice cream to tell the class they don't like it. They say *I don't like ice cream*. Do the same with cake, chocolate and bread.

Activity
- Point to the words on the board and say each one. Let the class repeat each word after you. Hold up each flashcard and say *bread, cake*, etc. The children look and repeat each word. Ask for four volunteers to come out and match the cards to the pictures/words.

- When they have done this, rub out the words underneath the pictures and ask for children to come and match the flashcard to the picture.

PB page 44
Ex. 1
- (L1) Explain to the class that they have to join the right word to the right picture. Go over 'chocolate' with them as the first example. Then go around each child and check that they can do the task. Help the ones who have problems.

PB page 44
Ex. 2
- (L1) Ask the children what Otto has in his tentacles. (Some cups.) Draw the 'u' shape on the board. Now tell the children that you will trace it in the air with your back to them. The children copy you with their forefingers. Tell them to trace on the desks, on their friends' backs, etc. Then they can trace the shape of the cups on the page. Next they can join the dots. Go around and help those with problems.

- Now tell them to trace with their forefingers over the 'u's on the page, and the 'u' in umbrella. Next they can, with their pencils, join the dots and write the word 'umbrella'. Finally the children can write the 'u's freehand in the space underneath. Remind the class to sit properly and hold their pencils correctly. Their books should be straight in front of them.

- When they have completed the 'u's, present 'y' in the same way. They can colour the shape with a yellow crayon.

Rhyme
- Play the rhyme that they will learn the next lesson. You may join in with the words. The children can sit and listen.

LESSON 3

New language	Known language	
	cake	bread
	chocolate	ice cream

Preparation
- Bring in some cake, some chocolate, some bread and a picture of some ice cream.

Revision
- Play 'Cops and Robbers'. Take the children into the playground. Divide the children into two teams – Cops and Robbers. Stand the groups behind lines facing one another. Put the bread, the cake, the chocolate and the picture of the ice cream on the ground about a third away from the Robbers to the Cops. (L1) Explain to the

children that you are going to shout out the name of an object. The Robbers then run and try to pick it up and take it back across their line. If the Cops touch them before they cross their line, they have to return their object. You may like to change the teams around after a while.

PB page 45
Ex. 3

- Explain to the class that the smiling face means that they like the food. The unhappy face means that they don't like it. (L1) Now explain that you are going to say a sentence and they have to listen. Then they must draw a happy or unhappy face on the page. Do the first example with them. Say:

  1) I like chocolate.
  2) I don't like fish.
  3) I don't like cake.
  4) I like ice cream.

  Say each sentence a few times before you go on to the next number. Go around while you are saying the sentences checking that the children are doing the exercise properly. Finally go over the whole exercise with the class.

- (L1) When they have done the exercise tell the children that they can draw the things that they like in the space at the bottom of the page. It can be food or drink. While they are doing this go around and encourage children to tell you what they like.

Rhyme

- Play the rhyme for the children to listen to and join in the words yourself. Let the children clap to it. Play it again and encourage them to join in with the words. Finally, let them say the rhyme with you.

  1 I like bread.
     I like jam.
     I like chocolate and fish.

  2 I like cake.
     I like eggs.
     I like ice cream in a dish.

Way in A: **Unit 12**

New language	Known language
an egg	
a hat	
a box	

Preparation
- Draw an egg, a box and a hat on the board, and label them.
- Make flashcards for egg, box, hat.
- You can also bring in an egg, a hat and a box.

Presentation
- Teach the new words, egg, box and hat. Either show the class an egg or point to the picture of an egg. Say *an egg*. Say it several times. Let the children repeat it after you. Now hold up a box or point to the picture. Say *a box* a few times. Let the children look at it and repeat *a box*. Show, or point to, a hat. Say *a hat* a few times. Let the children look at the object and repeat it after you.

- (L1) Explain to the children that you are going to point to one of the objects and you will say its name. If the object and the name is the same then they must repeat the word after you. For example, if you point to the box and say *a box* the children repeat *a box*. If you point to the box and say *an egg* they must remain silent or they are 'out'. Play this game at a quick pace. The last one in is the winner.

PB page 46
- Otto and Tubs find an egg. Otto decides to show Tubs a magic trick. He takes off his hat. What is going to happen? (L1) Tell the children to look at the top picture. Say *An egg*. Let the children repeat it after you several times. Now, looking at the bottom picture, say *A hat*. Again they repeat it a few times.

Practice
- Divide the class up into their groups. (L1) Explain that you will hold up or point to the egg and they must say it in their groups. Say *An egg*. Group 1 repeats it, then group 2, etc. Hold up or point to the hat and say *A hat*. Group 2 repeats it after you, then group 3, and so on.

- Ask if any of the class would like to come and act out the situation. Let as many as would like to come out.

A–Z
- Revise 'l' and 'k'. Point to your leg and say *leg*. Emphasize the initial sound /l/ and write 'l' on the board. Draw a kite quickly on the board and say *kite*. Emphasize the initial sound /k/ and write 'k'. Now write three more letters on the board: 'e', 'b' and 'h'. Say the sounds /e/, /b/ and /h/.

- (L1) Tell the class that you are going to say a sound and they have to come up and put a ring around the right letter. Divide the class into two teams, A and B. Say /e/ and a child from team A comes up and rings 'e'. Next say /b/ and a child from team B comes up, etc.

Activities
- Hold up a box and say *a box*. Show the flashcard only and say *box*. The children look at the card and say *box*. Do the same with 'egg' and 'hat'. Do it several times.

- (L1) Explain that you want three volunteers to come out and hold up the cards. Place the three children at the front of the classroom with the cards in their hands. Make sure that there is some distance between them. (L1) Tell the class that you are going to point to a picture/word on the board and they have to point to the child who has that flashcard. For example, point to the egg. Then the class must point to the child who is holding the flashcard 'egg'. Play this game several times.

- Now rub out the words underneath the pictures and continue with the game. Change the children who are holding up the cards.

- Tell the children to sit down and ask if any volunteer can come up and take a flashcard from you and match it to the correct picture on the board. Encourage them to say the word when they do so.

- Finally, if there is time, place the three flashcards on the floor. (L1) Explain that they are 'stones in a pond'. Ask if any child can hop from one 'stone' to the other and say the correct word. If they make a mistake, or cannot remember the word, then they will be eaten by the crocodile who lives in the pond around the stones.

LESSON 2

New language	Known language
It's in the . . .	a hat
	an egg

Preparation
- Bring in the flashcards for 'egg', 'hat' and 'box'.
- Bring in a hat, a box, an egg and a small box for each group.
- Draw these objects on the board.

Presentation
- Show the class the hat and say *a hat*. Put something in the hat, e.g. a pencil, and say *It's in the hat*. Show them that something is in the hat again and say *It's in the hat*. (L1) Check that they understand. Let the children repeat this a few times. Now put something (e.g. a piece of chalk) in the box and say *It's in the box*. Show them and say it again. Let the children repeat it several times.

PB page 47
- Otto has put the egg in his hat. Tubs is looking. The egg cracks open in the middle of the trick and a bird is in the egg. Otto is dismayed, but Tubs is delighted. (L1) Tell the class to look at the top picture. Say *It's in the hat*. Let them repeat this. Now, looking at the bottom picture say *It's in the egg*. Say it several times. Let the class repeat it.

Practice
- Divide the class into their groups. (L1) Tell them to look at the top picture. Say *It's in the hat* and group 1 repeats it, group 2, and so on. Looking at the bottom picture, say *It's in the egg*. Group 2 repeats it and so on, ending with group 1. Make sure that the children are looking at the correct picture when they are saying the sentence.

- (L1) Ask if any of the children would like to come out and act/mime the whole story. You will need three actors.

- Quickly give out a box to each group. (L1) Tell them that you are going to say one of two sentences. If you say *It's in the box* then they must put something (e.g. a pencil) in the box. If you say *It's in the egg* then they must point to the picture in their books. Do this a few times.

PB page 48
Ex. 1

• (L1) Tell the children that they are going to practise writing straight lines with Otto. Draw two or three straight lines on the board. With your back to the class trace several straight lines. Let the children copy you using their forefingers. They can trace them on their desks, etc.

• (L1) Tell them to look at the birds' legs at the top of the page. With their finger they can trace over the legs first and then join them with their pencils. Check their posture. Make sure that they are holding their pencils correctly and their books are straight.

• (L1) Now tell the children to trace over the 'i's with their fingers and the word 'in'. (L1) Check that they know the meaning of 'in'. They can then join the dotted 'i's and the word 'in'. Finally they can write them freehand. Go around and help individual children by showing each one how to form a letter. Make sure that each child is beginning at the top of each letter.

• Teach 'l' and 'k' in the same way.

Song

• If there is time at the end let the children listen to the song they will learn in the next lesson.

LESSON 3

New language	Known language	
	a hat	a cat
	an octopus	a boat
	an egg	an umbrella

Preparation

• Draw a hat, an octopus, an egg, a cat, a boat, and an umbrella on the board and write the words underneath.

• Make flashcards for hat, egg, umbrella.

Presentation

• (L1) Explain to the class that you are going to tell them to draw something on the board and the child who draws the best picture gets a point for his or her team. Divide the class into two teams, A and B. If there are more than twelve children in your class make three or four teams. (L1) Explain the meaning of the instruction *Draw a . . . .* Point to each picture on the board and say what it is. The children repeat the words after you. Now ask a child from each team to come out. (L1) Tell them that they have to draw the picture very quickly but the best picture gains a point for the team.

1) Draw a hat.
2) Draw an octopus.
3) Draw a cat.

4) Draw an egg.
5) Draw a boat.
6) Draw an umbrella.

PB page 49
Ex. 2

- (L1) Explain to the children that they have to listen to your instructions and that they must draw an object *in* something in the picture. Do an example with them first. Say *Draw a bird in the hat.* Go around and check their work. Now continue with the exercise.

  1) Draw a hat in the boat.
  2) Draw an egg in the umbrella.
  3) Draw an octopus in the egg.
  4) Draw a cat in the boat.

  Say each sentence several times. Go over the whole exercise with the class.

PB page 49
Ex. 3

- Point to each picture on the board and say *What's this?* Give the children the opportunity to answer. Now hold up the flashcards separately and let the children look at each one and say *hat, egg, umbrella.*

- (L1) Ask for some volunteers to come out and match a flashcard to the correct picture. Match the flashcards at least twice.

- (L1) Tell the class that in this exercise they must read the word and draw a picture of the object in the space provided in the book. Do the first example with them.

Song

- Play the song and join in with the words. The children can clap or hum to it. Play it again and encourage the children to sing the words. Play it a third time. Divide the class into two groups, one to sing the question and one to sing the reply.

  1   Where's my little cat?
      I'm here, I'm here.
      I'm in the hat.

  2   Where's my little mouse?
      I'm here, I'm here.
      I'm in the house.

LESSON 1

New language	Known language
nine	one–eight
a vine	a window

Preparation

- Bring in some soap liquid and something through which to blow bubbles.

- Make letter cards for 'v', 'w' and 'x'.

Revision

- You may like to take the children outside for this game or use an open area in the classroom. (L1) Explain the game to the children. They move around in a circle, they can sing if they like. Then you shout out a number, e.g. *Five!* Immediately the class has to form groups of five. Those who cannot form a group are out. Repeat this, varying the number, until there are only three children left. They are the winners.

Presentation

- Either use a numbers frieze or hold up nine fingers and count up to nine. Do it again. Let the class hold up nine fingers and count to nine after you. Hold up nine fingers and say 'nine' several times. Now the children do likewise.

- (L1) Tell the children that you are going to knock on the table and they have to tell you how many times you knocked. Knock 7, 9, 4 and 8 times.

- (L1) Now explain that you will say a number and they must clap the correct number of times, otherwise they are out. Practise all the numbers in this way.

PB page 50

- Belinda is blowing bubbles and enjoying herself. (L1) Ask the children if they ever blow bubbles. Count the number of bubbles together. Do this several times.

Practice

- Divide the children up into their groups. (L1) Tell group 1 to put on their Belinda puppets and count the bubbles, and then group 2, and so on.

- If you have brought in some soap liquid now blow some bubbles. (L1) Ask the different groups to count how many there are. Keep the numbers under ten!

A–Z

- Teach the letters 'v', 'w' and 'x'. (L1) Explain what a vine is. Say *vine*. Emphasize the initial sound and write 'v' on the board. Say /v/ and let the children look at the letter and repeat it after you. Point to the window and say *window*. Emphasize the initial sound /w/ and write 'w' on the board. Point to it and say the sound. Let the children look at 'w' and pronounce it. Now quickly sketch a box, or point to one in the classroom and say *box*. Pronounce the final sound /ks/, 'x'. Write 'x' on the board, point to it and pronounce it /ks/. Let the children look at it and pronounce it several times.

- Now give three volunteers the letter cards and ask them to match the card to one of the letters on the board. Do this several times so that the children who want to come out can do so. Encourage them to say the sound as they match the letter.

Activity

- Quickly hold up nine fingers, or point to the numbers frieze. Say *nine*. Write the numeral '9' on the blackboard and the word 'nine' underneath. Point to the word and say *nine*. Let the children look and say the word. (L1) Tell them that they will be reading that word in a later lesson.

Optional activity
- Take the children outside for this activity. (L1) Tell them to form a circle and join hands. Number the children off in 9's. Then you call out a number from 1–9, e.g. *Seven!* All the '7's then run clockwise around the outside of the circle and back to their places, without being touched by the '7' child behind. The player who has touched the largest number of other players is the winner. (If you have a small class you will have to use lower numbers.)

LESSON 2

New language	Known language
ten	one–nine

Preparation
- Bring in some soap liquid and something to blow through to make bubbles.

Presentation
- Either use a numbers frieze or hold up ten fingers and count from one to ten. Hold up ten fingers and say *ten*. Count from one to ten and let the class count with you. Do this several times.

PB page 51
- Belinda is very unhappy because she has soap up her nose. Do the children ever get soap up their noses? (L1) Tell them to count the number of bubbles. Count them together several times.

Practice
- Divide the class into their usual groups. (L1) Explain that they are going to put on their Belinda puppets and count the bubbles in their groups. Tell them to point to each one as they count it.

- (L1) Tell the class that you are going to blow some bubbles (or let a child do it). They must count, taking it in turns in their groups. First group 1 counts, then group 2 and so on. Blow a different amount of bubbles for each group to count. Again, don't go over ten!

PB page 52 Ex. 1
- (L1) Tell the class that they are going to draw the scales down Drago's back. First draw the pattern on the board. Then, with your back to the class, trace the shape in the air. (L1) Tell them to imitate you, using their forefingers. Let them trace it on their friends' backs, their desks, etc. After this, with their pencils, they can join the dots of Drago's scales from left to right.

- Now write 'v' on the board and trace it in the air with your back to the class. (L1) Tell the children to trace it – in the air, on their desks and over the shape on the page. (L1) Explain that the picture is of a vine. They can also join up the dots of the word 'vine' with their pencils. Check their posture, the position of their books and how they are holding their pencils. Then the children can write the letters and word 'vine' freehand.

- Teach 'w' and 'x' in the same way. Go around and help each child by showing how to form the letters on the page.

- Quickly hold up ten fingers and say *ten*. Write 10 on the board. Say *ten* again. Let the children copy you. Write 'ten' on the board and point to it and say *ten*. The children then look and say it several times. Tell them that they will be reading this in the next lesson.

LESSON 3	**New language**	**Known language**
		one–ten

Preparation
- Have enough small pieces of paper to cover each numeral in 'Number Bingo' on PB page 53.

- Write the numerals 7, 8, 9, 10 on the board and the names of the numbers underneath, e.g.   9
  nine

- Bring the ten cards with the numbers 1–10 on them, and their flashcards.

Revision
- (L1) Tell the class that when you point to a number on the board they must say the number. Point to the numbers at random.

- (L1) Explain to the children that you are going to hold up a flashcard and a volunteer can come out and match the flashcard to the right numeral on the blackboard. For example you hold up 'six' and a child comes out and matches it to '6'. Let ten volunteers do this. Now rub off the words on the board. (L1) Ask for volunteers to come up again and match the flashcards to the right numeral.

PB page 53
Ex. 2
- (L1) Tell the class that they have to help Tubs. They must count the objects and draw a line from the objects to the right numeral. They must also join the dots of the letters to form the number words. Do the first example with the class. Go around and check that the children are doing the exercise correctly.

PB page 53
Ex. 3
- You have played Bingo with letters in Unit 3, Lesson 3. This is the same game but using numbers, not letters. (L1) Explain this to the class.

- Let each group choose which card they want to play with – Drago's card, or Belinda's, etc. Give each group four pieces of plain paper. Put the numbers 1–10 in a bag. Pick a number from the bag. Hold it up. The first group to i) have the number on their card, and ii) say the number out loud, can cover over that number with a piece of plain paper. The first group to cover all the numbers is the winner. After playing the game once you may like to change cards around the groups.

Song
- Play the song and join in the words while the children hum it. Play it again and encourage the children to join in. Play it a third time and all sing it together. You may like to ask ten boys and girls to come out and mime being Indians.

One little, two little, three little Indians,
Four little, five little, six little Indians,
Seven little, eight little, nine little Indians,
Ten little Indian boys.

Ten little, nine little, eight little Indians,
Seven little, six little, five little Indians,
Four little, three little, two little Indians,
One little Indian girl.

Way in A: **Unit 14**

LESSON 1

New language	Known language
It's on the . . .	a cake
Where's the . . . ?	a book
a table	

Preparation
- Have ready the letter cards f, t, j, o, b, w and make a duplicate set of these six letters.

Presentation
- Teach the new items. Point to the table in the classroom and say *table*. Say it a few times. Let the class repeat it. Hold up a pencil, put it on the table and say *It's on the table*. Point to it and say it several times and let the children repeat it after you. Hold up a book and put it on the table. Point to it and say *It's on the table*. The children repeat this after you. Say it a few times. Then let them repeat the sentence in their groups. (L1) Check quickly that they have understood.

- (L1) Ask a child to come out and whisper in his or her ear to take the book off the table while you walk away. You walk around the classroom and look out of the window while the child does this. Come back and look puzzled. Say *Where's the book?* Say it several times. (L1) Tell the class to repeat it after you. They can repeat it in their groups too. Indicate to the child who removed the book to place it on the table and you can walk away again. When it is replaced suddenly turn and say *It's on the table*. The class then repeat it after you. Say it a few times and the children repeat it in their groups.

PB page 54
- Tubs is whispering into Belinda's ear asking where the cake is. It's Drago's birthday cake. Belinda says it's on the table. (L1) Tell the children to look at the top picture. Say *Where's the cake?* The class repeats this. Say it a few times and they repeat the question. Then say *It's on the table*. The class repeats this. Make sure that the children are looking at the top picture when they are saying the sentences. Now if they look at the bottom picture they can see the cake, in its box, on the table.

Practice
- Divide the class into two groups only at first, A and B. Remind the class to look at the pictures. (L1) Tell the children that group A will ask the question and group B will answer. Say *Where's the cake?* Group A puts on the Belinda puppets and repeats the question. Say *It's on the table*. Group B repeats the answer, wearing their Tubs puppets. Change the groups around so that group B asks the question and group A answers. Don't forget they must also change puppets. They must look at the pictures while they are speaking.

- At this point divide the class into their usual, smaller, groups. (L1) Explain that group 1 asks *Where's the cake?* and group 2 replies, *It's on the table*. Then group 2 asks group 3, and so on. They must look at the pictures while they ask and answer. Go around the groups a few times.

A–Z
- Revise 'f' and 't' and teach 'j'. Say *jump* and then do the action. Do it again. Point to the class and say *jump*. They must do the action. Point to a few individual children

66

and say *jump*. Emphasize the initial sound /dʒ/ and write 'j' on the board. Pronounce the sound again and let the children repeat it after you. Say it a few times.

- Hold up four fingers and say *four*. Emphasize the initial sound and write 'f' on the board. Let the children say the sound after you. Hold up two fingers and say *two*. Say /t/ and write 't' on the board. The children repeat the sound after you.

- Show the children the letter card 'j' and ask if any of them can come and match it to the right letter on the board.

Activity
- Now place the letter cards f, t, j, o, b, w on the desk in front of you. Gather the children around you for this game. Show them the cards, and say the sounds, pointing to each one, and they can repeat the sound after you. Show the duplicate set of letter cards to the class. Then lay *all* the cards face down so that no one can see them. (L1) Explain that you are going to pick two up and that you have to find a pair. If you find a pair then you can keep it. The player with the most number of pairs at the end of the game is the winner. Pick two cards. Do they match? If they don't match, you have to put the two cards back where they were face down. (L1) Ask a child to pick two now. Carry on with the game until all the cards are paired off. They should try to remember where the pair of the first card that they pick is, if, of course, it has previously been turned up. This is to train the children's memories.

LESSON 2

New language	Known language
a chair	It's on the . . .
	I'm . . .
	a cake

Preparation
- Bring in small boxes with lids on them, one for each group.

Revision
- Give out the boxes to each group. (L1) Explain to the children that you are going to say something is *in* or is *on* the box. If it is in the box then they must put an object (e.g. a pencil) in their box. If you say it is *on* the box then they must put it on the box (i.e. close the lid of the box and put the object on top). (L1) Tell them to do the action as quickly as possible. Say *It's on the box*. Then *It's in the box*. Say the two sentences several times and quicken the pace.

Presentation
- Teach the new item. Point to a chair and say *a chair*. Say it a few times and let the children repeat it after you. Sit on the chair and say *I'm on the chair*. Put a pencil or book on the chair and say *It's on the chair*. The children then put a pencil on their chair and say *It's on the chair*. They say it several times after you.

PB page 55
- Drago is coming. He'll see the cake! Belinda tries to hide it. She puts it on the chair and then she stands in front of it. Tubs sits on it! (L1) Now tell the class to look at the top picture. Say *It's on the chair*. Let the children repeat the sentence after you. Say it a few times and they repeat it. Looking at the bottom picture say *I'm on the cake*. (L1) Check that the class understand what Tubs is saying. Say it again and let the children repeat it several times.

Practice
- Divide the class up into their usual groups. While looking at the top picture say *It's on the chair*. (L1) Remind the children to look at the pictures. Group 1 repeats it, then group 2, and so on. Make sure that they are looking at the bottom picture. Say *I'm on the cake*. (L1) Tell them to pretend to be Tubs sitting on the cake. Let group 2 repeat it, then group 3, and so on.

- (L1) Ask if any three children want to come out and act the whole story. The children can put on the Belinda puppet when saying *It's on the chair* and the Tubs puppet when saying *I'm on the cake*.

PB page 56 Ex. 1
- (L1) Ask the children what Belinda has in her trunk. Tell them that they are going to draw more shapes. Write ⌐ on the board, then trace it in the air with your back to the class. They copy you using their forefingers by tracing the shape in the air, on their desks, etc. Do the same with the ⌐ shape. (L1) Now tell the children to join the dots together with their pencils. Go around and help them.

- Now show the children how to form 'f'. Draw it on the board. Trace it in the air with your back to the class. The children imitate you, using their forefingers, tracing it in the air, on their friends' backs, etc. Let them trace over the 'f' in their books and the word 'five'. Remind them to start at the large dot and cross the 'f' from left to right. (L1) Ask them what the word is. Now they can join the dots with their pencils. Check their posture and the position of their books is correct, and also check how they hold their pencils. Finally they can form a line of 'f's freehand and complete 'five'.

- Do the same with 'j' and 't'.

Song
- If there is time, let the children listen to the song that they will learn in the next lesson.

LESSON 3

New language	Known language	
It's in the . . .	a fish	
Where's the . . . ?	a leg	
a tree	a mouse	
a boat	a box	
a hand		

Preparation
- Draw a tree, a boat, a fish, a leg, a hand on the board and label them.

- Prepare flashcards for each word.

Revision
- Point to each picture on the board and say *What's this?* Give the children the opportunity to say what they are. Now you point to the picture of a tree and say *a tree* and the class repeats it after you. Do the same with the other pictures/words. Make sure that you are pointing to the picture as you say the word.

- Point to the picture of the tree and say *a tree*. Hold up a flashcard with 'tree' on it and say *tree*. The children look at the word and say it several times. Now point to the picture of the boat and say *boat*. Hold up the flashcard with 'boat' on it and say *boat*. Continue in this way with the other cards.

- (L1) Ask for five volunteers to come out and match a flashcard to a picture/word on the board. As they match them encourage them to say the word.

- Rub out the words under the pictures on the board. Again ask five volunteers to come out and match the cards to the pictures.

- If there is time play 'Stepping stones'. Put the flashcards down on the floor and gather the children around you. (L1) Explain that they must jump from one card, or 'stone', to the other and say the word as they do so. If they cannot read the word then they fall in the water and the crocodile eats them. Give every child who wants to the opportunity to play.

PB page 57 Ex. 2
- (L1) Explain to the children that they are going to match one half of a word to another. Go over the first one, 'tree', with them. Go around and help the ones who have difficulties. Go over the exercise with the whole class.

PB page 57 Ex. 3
- Write the numbers 1–10 at random on the board. Ask nine children, one by one, to come out and join up the numbers in the correct sequence. (L1) Ask the children what the animal is. Tell them to join up the numbers in the right order and then they will find out where the mouse is. Give them time to do the exercise and then say *Where's the mouse?* They should answer *It's in the box.*

Song
- Play the song to the class and join in the words while the children listen. Play it again and encourage them to sing the words. It may be easier to ask them just to sing the replies 'Here I am' and 'Very well, thank you'. Play it a third time. When the children say 'Here I am' they should hold up their thumb for 'thumb man'; their first finger for 'first man'; their middle finger for 'tall man'; their fourth finger for 'ring man' and their little finger for 'small man'. They make the finger 'run away' as they say the last lines of the verse.

1 Where is thumb man?
   Where is thumb man?
   Here I am.
   Here I am.
   How are you today, sir?
   Very well, I thank you.
   Run away.
   Run away.

2 Where is first man?

3 Where is tall man?

4 Where is ring man?

5 Where is small man?

Way in A: **Unit 15**

LESSON 1

New language	Known language
Happy Birthday	

Preparation
- Make letter cards for 'g', 'q' and 'z'.

Presentation
- (L1) Ask the children if any of them has had a birthday recently. What do they do on their birthday? Do they have a party? Who comes to the party?

PB page 58
- Drago is having a birthday party. Tubs is nibbling the cake. Drago is four so he has four candles on his cake. Drago is lighting the candles and Belinda is blowing them out! (L1) Tell the class that everyone is saying 'Happy Birthday!' to Drago. If there is a child in the class whose birthday it is say *Happy Birthday!* to her or him and get all the class to say it too.

- (L1) Tell the children to get their puppets out. First put Otto on one hand and Drago on the other. Make Otto say *Happy Birthday!* to Drago. Let the children repeat it after you. Then make Belinda say *Happy Birthday!* to Drago. The children can change their puppet to Belinda and say it too. Do the same with Tubs.

Practice
- Divide the children into their usual groups. Put the Tubs puppet on one hand and the Drago puppet on the other. Say *Happy Birthday!* to Drago and let group 1 repeat it after you, then group 2 and so on. Put Belinda on your hand instead of Tubs and say *Happy Birthday!* Group 2 repeats it after you, then group 3 and so on. Do the same with Otto. (L1) Tell the class that in the next lesson they will listen to a 'Happy Birthday' song they can sing to Drago.

A–Z
- Say *green* and emphasize the initial /g/. write 'g' on the board, say the sound and tell the children to repeat it after you. Say *question* and if necessary explain what a question is. Emphasize the initial /kw/ sound and write 'q' on the board. Ask the children to repeat the sound after you. Draw a picture of a zebra on the board and say *zebra*, emphasizing the initial /z/. Write 'z' on the board and ask the class to repeat the sound.

- (L1) Tell the class that you will say one of the sounds and volunteers can come up and point to the right letter.

- Give out the three letter cards and individual children can match them to the letters on the board.

Activities
- Now teach a new game called 'I can see something beginning with . . .' and you add a letter sound. (L1) Explain that you will say a sound and they have to guess what object it is. Make sure that you choose one that is in the room and that they know the English for it, e.g. window, door, book, etc. The first child to guess correctly can then choose a sound, saying, e.g. *I can see something beginning with f.* You may have to say the sentence for them and then they say the sound only.

- If there is time (L1) explain that at birthday parties games are usually played so that now the children can choose their favourite *Way in* game to play or sing their favourite song from *Way in*.

LESSON 2	**New language**	**Known language**	
	I'm . . .	five	
	three	six	
	four		

Preparation • Bring in ten stones.

Revision • (L1) Explain to the children that you have some stones and that you are going to put a few of them in your hand and they have to guess how many there are. The first child to guess correctly can come up and be 'teacher' and put a number of stones in his or her hand.

Presentation • Tubs is three years old and Drago is four years old. (L1) Tell the children to look at Tubs. Say that you are all going to pretend to be Tubs. Say *I'm three*. Let the children repeat it. Say it a few times. (L1) Now tell them that you are all going to pretend to be Drago. Say *I'm four*. Let the children repeat this after you. Do this several times.

Practice • Tell the class to take out their Tubs and Drago puppets. Divide the class up into their usual groups. Hold up Tubs and say *I'm three*. Group 1 holds up the puppet and says *I'm three*, then group 2, and so on. Now hold up Drago and say *I'm four*. Group 2 holds up Drago and says *I'm four*. The groups say the sentence in turn.

• (L1) Ask if any of the class want to come out and be Tubs or Drago. They can say *I'm four* and then the class can guess *Drago*. Or they say *I'm three* and the class guess *Tubs*.

• (L1) Ask the children how old they are and tell those who are four to stand up and say *I'm four*. Then the children who are five can stand up and say *I'm five*. They repeat it after you. If there are any older or younger children say their age for them to repeat it.

PB page 60 Ex. 1 • Here the children have to complete the dotted lines of the fringe and handle on Tubs' umbrella. This will help them in the formation of the letters 'g' and 'q'. First demonstrate the movements in the air, with your back to the class and let the children imitate you. Then ask them to trace the shapes with their fingers, first on their desks, then in their books. Finally they join the dots in pencil.

• Show the children how to form the letter 'g' on the board. Then trace it in the air with your finger and let the children copy you. Then they trace over the letter in their books using their forefingers. Finally they join the dots in pencil and then copy the letters and the word freehand in their books.

• Teach 'q' and 'z' in the same way.

Song • If there is time let the children listen to the song that you'll teach them in the next lesson.

LESSON 3

New language	Known language	
a table	a cat
a leg	a tree
an ear	a tail
a boat	red
a nose	one–ten

Preparation

• Draw a table, a tail, an ear, a leg on the blackboard and write the words underneath. Bring in flashcards for those words, and also for cat, tree and nose.

• Bring in all the twenty-six letter cards.

• At another end of the board write the letters 't', 'f', 'o', 'b', 'a', 's'.

Activities

• Give out the letter cards to the class. (L1) Explain to the children that you are going to point to a word that they know e.g. 'leg' and that those who have the same letters as the word on the board have to come out to the front of the classroom and stand in a line. They have to stand in the right order with their cards so that they form the word 'leg'. The class can then say the word 'leg'. If you have a small class give two or three cards to each child. Use the following words:
1) red 2) table 3) ear 4) cat 5) boat 6) tail 7) four 8) grey 9) hand 10) jump 11) kite 12) six 13) vine 14) window 15) zebra. You do not have to use all of these words, but they cover all twenty-six letters of the alphabet. When the class begins to lose interest change the activity. (You may want to change the vowel cards around during the game so that the same children don't come up all the time.)

• (L1) Tell the class that you are going to say a sound of a letter that they know. It will be one of the letters on the board. You will say it and then they have to write it down.
Say *1) /b/; 2) /a/; 3) /s/; 4) /o/; 5) /t/.*
Go around and check the children's work as you say the sounds. Say them several times. Finally go over the exercise with the whole class.

• Now point to each picture/word on the board and say *What's that?* Give the children the opportunity to tell you. Now hold up the flashcards for each picture and say the word, e.g. *table*. The children look at the flashcard and say *table*. Do the same with the other words. (L1) Ask if any child would like to come out and match the flashcard to the picture on the board. Do this with all the flashcards and encourage the children to say the word when they match it.

• Rub out the words underneath the pictures on the board. Volunteers can come out and match the flashcard to the picture. Do this with all the flashcards several times.

PB page 61
Ex. 2

- (L1) Explain to the class how to fill in the crossword puzzle. Do 'table' with them. Make sure that the flashcards are displayed so that the children can copy the words if they need to.

PB page 61
Ex. 3

- Point to a tree or quickly draw one on the board. Say *a tree*. Hold up the flashcard with 'tree' on it and say *tree*. Let the children look at it and say *tree*. Do the same with the other words.

- (L1) Now explain that Belinda is trying to cross the pond without falling in. She needs help, therefore, to read the words. Can the children help? Let them read the words in pairs. Go around and listen to them read and check their understanding of the words.

- (L1) Explain that Drago is trying to add up on his fingers and toes. Can they help him? Do one sum on the board with the class. Write '1 + 2 = ' and say as you write *one and two*. Wait for the answer from the class, *three*. (L1) Tell them to complete the sums. Go around and help those who have problems.

Song

- Play the 'Happy Birthday' song to the class and join in the words. Play it again and encourage the children to join in. Play it a third time. You may like to choose a few children to sing the 'Drago' verse on their own.

  1 We wish you a Happy Birthday,
     We wish you a Happy Birthday,
     We wish you a Happy Birthday,
     You're four today.

  2 I'm four today,
     Yes, I'm four today.
     Today's my birthday,
     And I'm four today.

  3 We wish you a Happy Birthday,
     We wish you a Happy Birthday,
     We wish you a Happy Birthday,
     You're four today.

Way in B: **Unit 1**

LESSON 1

New language	Known language
My name's . . .	Hallo.

Preparation
- Make sure everyone has their puppets.

Revision
- Greet the children. Say *Hallo*. The class replies, *Hallo*. Greet a few individual children and they reply. (L1) Tell the class to say *Hallo* to the person next to them, behind them, etc.

Presentation
- Point to yourself and say *My name's* . . . . Do this a few times. (L1) Check that the children have understood.

PB page 2
- Here the children meet their new friend, Pam. She is resting on a 'rock', but the 'rock' is Belinda! Both are surprised. Pam introduces herself. (L1) Check that the children understand the situation. (L1) Ask them if they like Pam. (L1) Ask them to look at the first picture again. You are all going to pretend to be Belinda. Say *Hallo*. Let the children repeat this after you. Next, looking at the bottom picture, pretend to be Pam. Say *My name's Pam*. Let the children repeat it after you. Do this several times.

Practice
- Divide the class into small groups. (L1) Tell them to take out their Belinda puppets. You pretend to be Pam and make the Belinda puppet greet you: *Hallo*. Then you reply *Hallo* to Belinda. Let group 1 imitate you, then group 2, and so on. Now pretend to be Pam again, point to yourself and say *My name's Pam*. Do this a few times. (L1) Remind the class that they are pretending to be Pam. Let group 2 point to themselves and repeat the sentence after you, then group 3, and so on.

- (L1) Explain to the class that two children can come out and pretend to be Pam and Belinda. Belinda says *Hallo* and Pam says *My name's Pam*. Do this with as many children as want to.

- (L1) Now ask if some of the class would like to come out and say who they are. When they come out whisper in their ear *My name's (Anna)*. Then they say the sentence out aloud. Let as many as want to come out.

Activities
- For this game take the children outside or use an open area in the classroom. Sit the children on the ground in a circle. (L1) Explain to them that one child stands up and walks around the outside of the circle. He or she stops next to any other child and says *Hallo*. The two children then run around the circle in opposite directions. When they meet they shake hands and say to each other *Hallo*. They then carry on running to see who gets back to the empty seat first. The child who is left standing then starts again.

- If there is time the children can draw a picture of Pam. When they have finished you can display all of the pictures on the classroom wall.

LESSON 2	**New language**	**Known language**
	What's your name?	My name's . . .

Preparation
- Write each child's name on a card for them to copy.

Revision
- Point to yourself and say *My name's* . . . . (L1) Ask if any of the children want to stand up and say who they are.

Presentation
- (L1) Ask four children to volunteer to come out to the front. Close your eyes and turn around and, still with your eyes closed, touch a child and say *What's your name?* Try and guess once, e.g. *Anna?* Then the child must answer *My name's* . . . . Open your eyes. The children can switch around and you close your eyes again and touch one of them saying *What's your name?* Try and guess the name. Then the one touched answers *My name's* . . . .

PB page 3
- Pam and Belinda are shaking hands/trunks. Pam is asking Belinda what her name is. Belinda introduces herself. (L1) Check that the class understand. (L1) Ask the class if they think the two will be friends. Looking at the top picture, pretend to be Pam and say *What's your name?* Ask the question a few times. Let the children also pretend to be Pam and repeat it after you. Do this a few times. Now pretend to be Belinda. While looking at the last picture say *My name's Belinda*. Let the children repeat this. (L1) Remind them to look at the pictures when they say the sentences.

Practice
- (L1) Tell the class to take out their Belinda puppet. First everyone pretends to be Pam. Speak to the Belinda puppet and ask it *What's your name?* Let group 1 ask the question, then group 2, and so on. Hold up the puppet and answer *My name's Belinda*. Group 2 repeat this and hold up Belinda, then group 3, and so on.

- (L1) Now tell the class that group 1 will pretend to be Pam and ask the question, and group 2 will hold their Belinda puppet and reply. Then group 2 pretends to be Pam and asks the question and group 3 will reply, and so on.

- (L1) Ask if any of the children want to come out and be Pam and Belinda. They can act out the whole scene, both pages.

PB page 4
Ex. 1
- (L1) Explain to the children that they have to draw a picture of themselves in the space. They can colour it in. Go around while they are doing this. Praise and encourage them.

- (L1) Explain that the whole class must watch you writing a sentence on the board. Write 'My name's . . .'. Say the words. (L1) Tell the children to trace over the words on the page with their forefinger. They must start at 'M' and continue tracing from left to right.

- Give out the cards with their names on. (L1) Explain that they must copy their name into the space provided in the book. Let them join up the dots and then write in their name. Go around and help those who have difficulties.

Optional activity	● Take the children out into the playground or use an open area in the classroom. (L1) Explain that this is a chasing game. One person is blindfolded and has to run and catch another person. When he or she is caught the 'blind person' has to say *What's your name?* The child caught makes a noise, squeaks, etc. and the 'blind person' has to guess who it is. If he or she is right then the person caught becomes the 'blind' player.
Song	● If there is time, play the song that the children will learn in the next lesson.
Further suggestions	● Play 'Mr and Mrs Noah' (*Bonanza* p. 157–159). Change the language to 'What's your name?' and a player mimes one of the five *Way in* characters.

LESSON 3

New language	Known language
a cat	a boat
a book	a cake

Preparation	● Draw pictures of a cat, a book, a boat, a cake on the board. Label them underneath. ● Prepare flashcards for each word. ● Write a A b B c C on the board.
PB page 5 Ex. 2	● Point to the letters on the board and explain to the children that each small letter has a 'big friend'. Explain that the big letters are used for starting people's names and for starting sentences. With your back to the class trace each letter in the air. Say the sound at the same time. Let the class copy you using their forefingers.
	● Now let the children trace over the letters on the page with their fingers. Then they can join the dots together to form the letters with their pencils. (L1) Remind them to hold their pencils correctly and check their posture.
	● Tell the children that all letters have names as well as sounds. The children already know the sounds. Point to a A, b B and c C on the board and ask the class to say the sounds. Then explain that they are going to learn the names of these letters. Point to the letters again and say their sounds and their names: a /eɪ/; b /biː/; c /siː/. Let the children repeat them after you a few times.
	● Now tell the class to do the second part of the exercise in their books. They have to find a small letter that matches its 'big friend'. Go over the first one with the class. (L1) Ask them to look for a big and a small C. Join c to C. Go around and check that the children understand and are doing the exercise properly.
Activity	● Point to the pictures of the cat, etc. on the board and say *What's this?* Give the children the opportunity to answer. Hold up the flashcard and say *cat* and let the children look at the flashcard and say the word. Do the same with the other flashcards.
	● (L1) Ask for volunteers to come out and match the flashcards to the pictures/words.

● When this has been done rub out the words under the pictures and ask for children to come out again and match a flashcard to a picture.

**PB page 5
Ex. 3**

● Show the class how to do the first example. (L1) Explain that they must look at the picture of the cat, then find the missing part of the word. When they have found it they must draw a line from it to the picture and write the missing letters under the picture. Let them do the others on their own. Go around and help individual children. Go over the exercise with the whole class.

Song

● Play the song for the children to listen to and join in with the words. Play it again and let the children hum or encourage them to join in. Play it a third time and everyone can sing it together.

1	Two little dicky birds, Sitting on a wall.	*(Hold up the forefinger of each hand.)*
	My name's Peter.	*(Waggle one finger.)*
	My name's Paul.	*(Waggle the other finger.)*
2	Fly away, Peter.	*(Take away the first finger.)*
	Fly away, Paul.	*(Take away the second finger.)*
	Come back, Peter.	*(Bring back the first finger.)*
	Come back, Paul.	*(Bring back the second finger.)*

Way in B: **Unit 2**

LESSON 1

New language	Known language
This is . . .	

Revision
- Hold up a book and say *This is a book*. Let the children repeat it after you. Quickly point to different objects in the classroom: a door, a table, a chair and say *This is a door*, etc. Let the children repeat the sentences after you.

Presentation
- Point to a child in the class and say *This is (Maria)*. Do this several times with different children. Let the children listen at this point.

PB page 6
- Belinda is taking Pam to meet her friends. She introduces her to Drago and Otto. (L1) Check that the class understands. (L1) Ask the class who they can see in the top picture. How does Otto greet Pam in the bottom picture? Would they like to shake hands with an octopus?! (L1) Tell them to look at the top picture. Let everyone pretend to be Belinda. Say *This is Drago*. Let the children repeat the sentence after you. Do this a few times. While looking at the bottom picture say *This is Otto*. Let the children look at the picture and say *This is Otto*. Repeat this several times.

Practice
- Hold up the Drago puppet and introduce him. Say *This is Drago*. The children hold up their puppets. Group 1 repeat it after you and then the other groups in turn. Now hold up the Otto puppet. Say *This is Otto*. Let group 2 hold up their Otto puppet and repeat it after you, then group 3, etc.

- (L1) Ask if four children would like to come out and act the situation.

- (L1) Ask one of the groups to come up to the front. Take each child in turn and introduce him or her to another child saying *This is (Suzanna)*. They shake hands. (L1) Tell the class that in their groups they must take it in turns for one of them to introduce another to the group as you have done, saying, *This is . . . .* Then they shake hands.

Activity
- Give out a piece of plain paper to each child. (L1) Explain that they can draw one of the characters, either Drago or Otto, being introduced by Belinda. They can colour in the characters and while they are doing this you can go around and write under each picture either 'This is Drago' or 'This is Otto'. When they have all finished display the pictures around the classroom wall. Ask the class whether any of them would like to go up to their picture and say *This is (Drago)*.

LESSON 2

New language	Known language
	This is . . .

Revision
- (L1) Tell the class that you are going to hold up a puppet and they have to hold up the same puppet and say *This is . . .* and name the puppet. Hold up Drago and then Otto. They hold up theirs and say *This is Drago*. Then, *This is Otto*.

Presentation PB page 7

- Belinda continues to introduce her friends to Pam. Finally she introduces Pam to everyone. (L1) Ask the children who they can see in the top picture. (L1) Check that they understand that Belinda is introducing Pam to everyone. (L1) Ask them to look at the top picture again. Pretend to be Belinda and say *This is Tubs*. Let the children look at the picture and repeat it after you a few times. Now they can look at the bottom picture. Say *This is Pam*. Let the children say it after you. Say it a few times and let them repeat it.

Practice

- Hold up the Tubs puppet and say *This is Tubs*. Let group 1 repeat it after you, then group 2, etc. Select a girl from the class and tell the children to pretend that she is Pam. Introduce her, saying *This is Pam*. Group 2 repeats it after you, then group 3 and so on.

- (L1) Ask if five children want to come out and act the characters and introduce each other. Let as many as wish to come out and act the situation.

PB page 8 Ex. 1

- (L1) Explain to the class that each section has some jigsaw pieces in it and those pieces make one of the characters. They have to look carefully at them and decide which animal it is. Then they have to write the name of who it is underneath. Go through the first one with the class: *This is Drago*. The capital letters are given in dotted form, as the children have not learned how to write them yet. When they begin to write check their posture, that their books are straight and that they are holding their pencils correctly.

Song

- Play the song to the class that they will learn in the next lesson.

LESSON 3

New language	Known language	
four	a fish	
a door	an egg	

Preparation

- Draw the numeral '4' and pictures of a door, a fish, and an egg on the board. Label them underneath.
- Prepare a flashcard for each word.
- Write d D, e E, f F on the board.

PB page 9 Ex. 2

- Point to d D, e E, and f F on the board and say their sounds. Then trace the capital letters in the air with your back to the class, saying the sounds at the same time. The children copy you using their forefingers.

- (L1) Tell the children to look at their books and trace over the letters at the top of the page with their fingers. Then they can join the dots and form the letters. Go around and help them.

- (L1) Ask the children if they remember the names of the letters that they learnt in the previous lesson. Give them the opportunity to tell you. If they can tell you, write up the letters as they say them. If they are unable to say them, encourage them to tell you the letter sounds, then write A, B, C on the board and say the names of the letters. The children can repeat the names after you. Now point to d D, e E and f F on the board and teach their names: d /diː/; e /iː/; f /ef/. Let the children repeat the names after you.

- (L1) Now tell the children that you will say a letter name and you want one of them to come up and put a ring round the correct letter. Do this a few times with D, E and F and then include A, B and C.

- (L1) Explain that in the second part of this exercise the children have to look at the small letter outside the circle and find its 'big friend' inside. Do the first one, 'c' with the whole class. Go around and help them. Ask individual children to point to the letters and say their sounds and names, but only of the letters that they have learnt.

PB page 9
Ex. 3

- Before you begin the exercise point to each picture on the board and say *What's this?* Give the children the opportunity to tell you. Now hold up the flashcards one by one, and say the words: *four, fish, door, egg.* The class repeat them after you. Make sure they are looking at the word as they say it.

- (L1) Ask for volunteers to come up and match the flashcard to the picture/word on the board. When four children have done this rub out the words and ask some other children to match the cards to the pictures.

- (L1) Explain to the class that in their books there are four dotted pictures. They have to join the dots to find out what they are. Then they read the four words at the top and copy the right word inside the right picture. Go around and help individual children.

Song and
rhyme

- Play the rhyme for the children to listen to and join in the words. Play the rhyme again and encourage the children to join in. Play it a third time and all say it together.

A, B, C, D, E, F, G,
H, I, J, K, L, M,
N, O, P, Q,
R, S, T, U,
V, W, X, Y, Z.
A is for apple.
B is for book.
C is for cake.
D is for door.
E is for elephant.
F is for four.

LESSON 1

New language	Known language
I can . . .	jump
swim	
fly	

Preparation • Make three flashcards: 'I can jump', 'I can swim', 'I can fly'.

Presentation • Jump up and down and stop and say *I can jump*. It is important to stop so that 'I can jump' is not confused with 'I am jumping'. Do the action again and then stop and say *I can jump*. Gesture to the children to jump and you jump too. (L1) Check that they understand the sentence. Say *I can jump* and let them repeat it after you. Do this a few times. Now pretend to swim. Say *I can swim*. Say it a few times. The children can pretend to swim and repeat the sentence *I can swim*.

• (L1) Tell the children that you are going to do one of the actions and say a sentence, either *I can swim* or *I can jump*. If the action and the sentence match, the class do the action. If your action and the sentence *don't* match, then they don't do either action. Do this a few times. Now pretend to fly, then say *I can fly*. Say it several times. (L1) Tell the children to pretend to fly. Then they say after you *I can fly*. Do this a few times. Play the game again including *I can fly*.

PB page 10 • Otto and Drago are showing off to Pam. Otto is saying he can swim and Drago that he can fly. (L1) Ask the children who is in the top picture. What is Otto doing? What is Drago doing in the bottom picture? (L1) Tell the children to look at Otto. Pretend to be the octopus and say *I can swim*. Let the children repeat the sentence after you. Do this a few times. Looking at the bottom picture, pretend to be Drago. Say *I can fly*. The children repeat after you. Do this a few times.

Practice • (L1) Tell the children to take out their Drago and Otto puppets. Hold up your Otto puppet, pretend to make it swim and say *I can swim*. Let group 1 repeat this after you, then group 2, etc. Hold up your Drago puppet, pretend to make it fly and say *I can fly*. Group 2 repeats it after you, then group 3, etc.

• (L1) Ask the children if anyone wants to come out with their puppets and say the sentences.

• (L1) Now ask the children to tell you truthfully who can swim. These children say after you *I can swim*. (L1) Ask if anybody can fly. No!

Activity • Jump up and down. Say *I can jump*. Show the class the flashcard and say *I can jump*. They look at it, and repeat the sentence. (L1) Tell them to jump and say it. Pretend to swim, and say *I can swim*. Show the children the flashcard and say *I can swim*. The children look and repeat it. Then they mime swimming. Pretend to fly and say *I can fly*. Hold up the flashcard and say *I can fly*. The class look and repeats it after you. They then mime flying.

• Now play a game. (L1) Explain to the children that you are going to show them a flashcard. They have to read it and do the action as quickly as possible. The last to do the action is 'out'. Use the flashcards 'I can jump', 'I can swim' and 'I can fly'. Play the game a few times and quicken the pace.

LESSON 2	**New language**	**Known language**
	run	I can . . .

Preparation
● Make a flashcard: 'I can run'.

Revision
● (L1) Explain to the children that you are going to do an action and say *I can . . . .* If the action and what you say is true then they repeat the sentence. If it is not true, then they are silent.

 1) Pretend to swim and say *I can jump.*
 2) Pretend to fly and say *I can fly.*
 3) Jump and say *I can swim.*
 4) Jump and say *I can jump.*
 5) Pretend to fly and say *I can swim.*
 6) Pretend to swim and say *I can swim.*

Presentation
● Run to the door. Stop and say *I can run.* Do it again, then say it. Quickly find an open space and let the children run. Then stop them and they say *I can run.*

PB page 11
● Belinda is showing off to Pam. She's shouting that she can run. She doesn't see the seaweed and she slips and falls. (L1) Check that the class understand. (L1) Tell them to look at the top picture. Pretend to be Belinda and say *I can run.* Say it again and let the class repeat it after you.

Practice
● Hold up your Belinda puppet and say *I can run,* (L1) Tell the class to hold up their Belinda puppets. Let group 1 repeat it after you, group 2, and so on.

● (L1) Ask if three children would like to come out with the Drago, Belinda and Otto puppets and say the sentences.

● Quickly hold up the flashcard 'I can run'. Say the sentence and let the children look at it and say it and do the action.

PB page 12
Ex. 1
● (L1) Explain to the children that you are going to pretend to be the different characters. They have to listen to you, then look at the picture and decide if what you say is true or false. If it seems true then the children put a tick. If the sentence seems false then they put a cross. Do the first one with them.

 1) I can jump. √
 2) I can fly. ×
 3) I can swim √
 4) I can run. ×

Say the sentences several times to give the children the opportunity of getting the answers right. Go over it with the whole class.

PB page 12
Ex. 2

- (L1) Ask the class if they can all run. Here they can draw themselves running. They can draw clothes and colour them in.

- When they have completed the drawing they must look at you. Write 'I can run' carefully on the board. Say it as you write it. Tell the children to trace over the words with their forefingers in the book and then join the dots together underneath. Finally they can write the sentence freehand. Go around and ask each child to read the sentence to you. Help individual children to form the letters.

Song

- If there is time let the class listen to the song that they will learn next lesson.

LESSON 3

New language	Known language
	a head
	a hand
	an ice cream

Preparation

- Prepare flashcards for 'ice cream', 'head', 'hand'.

- Bring in a picture of an ice cream.

- Write g G, h H, i I on the board.

PB page 13
Ex. 3

- (L1) Ask the children to look carefully at each small letter and its big one on the board. Then with your back to the class trace each capital letter in the air, saying its sound. Let the children copy you, using their forefingers.

- (L1) Tell the class to trace over the shape of the letters in their books, using their fingers. Then they can join the dots with their pencils to form the letters. Go round and check their posture.

- Now tell the children that they are going to learn the names of these letters. Point to each letter and say its sound first, then its name: g /dʒiː/; h /eitʃ/; i /ai/.

- (L1) Explain that in the second part of the exercise in their books the children have to look at the small letters on the left and 'find a friend' among the line of letters to the right of them. Go over 'g' with them. Go around and help individual children. Encourage them to tell you the sound and the name of each letter.

PB page 13
Ex. 4

- First show the class a picture of an ice cream. Ask *What's this?* and give them the opportunity to tell you. Hold up the flashcard and say *ice cream*. The class repeat it. Point to your head and say *What's this?* Let the children answer *head*. Hold up the flashcard and say *head*. Hold up your hand and ask *What's this?* The class answer *hand*. Show them the flashcard and say *hand*. They look and repeat *hand*.

- (L1) Now ask the children to look at the picture of Pam in their books. What are the arrows pointing to? They must look at the words at the bottom of the page, and then write the correct words next to the arrows. Do the first one with them. Go around and help individual children, especially the slower ones.

Song
- Play the song through and join in with the words while the children listen. Play it again and encourage them to join in. You may like to play it line by line and let them repeat it. Play it a third time all the way through. 'Abracadabra wizzy woo' is a magic word!

      Abracadabra wizzy woo,
      I can fly and so can you.
      Abracadabra wizzy woo,
      I can fly and so can you.
      I can fly,
      I can run,
      I can swim,
      I can jump,
      I can run,
      I can swim,
      I can fly and so can you.

Way in B: **Unit 4**

LESSON 1

New language	Known language
One hen	one–four
Two eggs	

Preparation
- Bring in a picture of a hen and two eggs or draw them on the board.
- Write 1 one, 2 two, 3 three and 4 four on the board.
- Make flashcards for 'one', 'two', 'three', 'four'.

Revision
- Say a number from 1 to 4 and a child comes and points to it on the board. Remember to praise children when they get it right.
- Show them the flashcard 'one' and say *one*. Let the class repeat it. Do the same with the other flashcards. Ask for four volunteers to come up and match the card to the number/word on the blackboard. If they do this successfully rub out the words and ask for four children to match the cards to the numbers alone.
- Play 'Jumping the line'. Draw a line on the floor. One side is true, the other false. Hold up a flashcard and say a number. If it is true then the children jump to the true side. If it is untrue then they jump to the false side. Show the flashcards twice each.

Presentation
- Teach the new items. Point to the picture of a hen and say *a hen*. Say it a few times. Let the children repeat it after you several times. Show the class an egg and say *What's this?* Give them the opportunity to say *an egg*. Hold up – or point to – the eggs. Say *eggs*. (NB the pronunciation is /egz/.) Let the children look at them and say *eggs*. Hold up two and say *two eggs*. They repeat this after you, several times.

PB page 14
- Drago is reading a cookery book. Pam and Tubs are looking at the hen. She lays two eggs. (L1) Check that the children understand the situation. (L1) Ask the class who is in the top picture. What are Pam and Tubs doing? What is Drago reading? The class can now look at the bottom picture. (L1) Ask what has the hen laid? (L1) Tell them to look at the top picture, at the hen. Say *One hen*. (L1) Check that they understand. Say it again and let the children repeat it. Do this a few times. Looking at the bottom picture, say *Two eggs*. Say it again and let the children repeat it.

Practice
- (L1) Tell the children to look at the pictures again. Say *One hen* and group 1 repeats it, then group 2, and so on. Make sure that the class are looking at the right picture. Say *Two eggs*. Group 2 repeats it, then group 3, etc.
- (L1) Ask if any of the class wants to come out and act out the situation. One child can be the hen.

Activities
- Play the game 'How many teeth, Mr (or Mrs) Bear?' (L1) First explain the title to the children. Point to your teeth and say *teeth*. Then say *How many teeth?* Let the class repeat this question a few times. Find an open area in the classroom or take the children out to the playground. Choose a child to be 'Mr Bear', or 'Mrs Bear'. Sit the child in the middle of a large circle drawn on the floor. The rest of the children

can now enter the circle and ask 'How many teeth Mr/s Bear?' The bear gives a bad-tempered answer in a low voice e.g. *Two*. If he or she says any number except ten, they are safe but if he or she says *Ten!* all the children must run outside the circle very quickly. If the bear catches one of them in the circle that child becomes Mr/s Bear.

● If there is time tell the class to listen to you and draw what you say.

1) Draw one book.
2) Draw two eggs.
3) Draw one box.
4) Draw two tables.

Say these sentences a few times to give the children time to draw the pictures correctly.

LESSON 2

New language	**Known language**
Three lemons.	
Four cakes.	

Preparation
● Bring in three lemons, and four cakes or a picture of them.

● Draw lemons, cakes, hens and a book on the board.

● Write 1 one, 2 two, 3 three, 4 four on the board.

● Prepare flashcards for 'hens', 'lemons', 'cakes', 'book'.

Presentation
● Show the children a lemon. Say *a lemon*. Let the children repeat it after you. Say it several times. Show the children two lemons and say *lemons*. The children look and repeat *lemons* a few times. Count the lemons you have: *One, two, three lemons*. Let the children say this after you. Now point to a picture or show a cake. Ask the class *What's this?* They answer *A cake*. Show several cakes. Say *cakes*. The children repeat this after you. (L1) Check that they understand. Count the number of cakes: *One, two, three, four cakes*. Let the children repeat this after you. (NB The final sound in 'cakes' is an /s/ sound. In 'lemons' it is /z/.)

PB page 15
● In the top picture Belinda is stirring some mixture and Pam is picking lemons. They are helping Drago to make something. In the bottom picture Drago's cakes are finished. Everyone is ready for a picnic but there are four cakes and five people! (L1) Check that the children understand the situation. Tell them to count the number of cakes and the number of people at the picnic.

● (L1) Tell the children to look at the top picture. Count the lemons: *One, two, three*. Say *Three lemons*. Make sure the children are looking at the lemons. They count them and repeat *Three lemons*. They say this several times. While looking at the bottom picture, count the cakes: *One, two, three, four*. Say *Four cakes*. Let the class look at the cakes, count them and repeat *Four cakes* a few times.

- (L1) Ask the children what they think Belinda is doing in the top picture. What is Pam trying to pick? How is Tubs feeling? Looking at the bottom picture, ask the children to count the number of cakes. Then they can count the number of characters.

Practice
- Divide the class up into their usual groups. (L1) Tell them to look at the lemons. Say *Three lemons* and group 1 repeats it, then group 2 and so on. Now tell them to look at the cakes. Say *Four cakes*. Group 2 repeats it after you, then group 3, and so on.

PB page 16 Ex. 1
- First point to the numerals on the board and allow the children to say *one, two, etc.* Point to the lemons, hold up the flashcard 'lemons' and say *lemons*. Let the class look at the card and say *lemons*. Do this a few times. Point to the cakes, hold up the card 'cakes' and say *cakes*. Let the children repeat this after you. Do the same with the other flashcards.

- (L1) Now ask for volunteers to come up and match the cards to the pictures.

- (L1) Ask the children to look at their books and explain that in this exercise they have to read the caption and draw the object/s in the space provided. Do one example with the class first. Go around and check that the children are doing the exercise correctly.

PB page 16 Ex. 2
- (L1) Tell the class that you are going to play a game. Divide them into two teams, A and B. (L1) Explain that you are going to give them two numbers and they must add them up. If they are right then they gain a point for their team. Pick one player at a time, first one from team A, then team B, and so on.

  1) 1 and 3
  2) 2 and 2
  3) 1 and 1
  4) 3 and 1

  You can include higher numbers if you like.

- (L1) Now tell the class that Drago needs some help adding up the sums in the book. Go around and help each child individually.

Song
- If there is time let the class listen to the song that they will learn next lesson.

LESSON 3

New language	Known language	
tree	leg	
kite	lemon	
ladder	jump	
plane	swim	

Preparation
- Draw pictures on the board of a tree, kite, ladder, plane, leg and lemon, and also stick figures illustrating 'jump' and 'swim'. Label them.

- Write j J, k K, l L on the board.

- Bring in two clothes pegs.

- Make letter cards for A, B, C, D, E, F, G, H.

Revision
- Play 'Dance of the Ostriches'. Either use an open area in the classroom or go into the playground. Divide the class into two teams. Select one child from each team and stand them facing each other, ready to begin. Attach a letter card to the back of each child, using the clothes pegs. Put the children's hands behind their backs. They must dance around each other and try to see the letter on the other child's back. Give a point to the child who says the *name* of the letter. Then it is the turn of the next children in the teams. The first team to get (3) points is the winner.

PB page 17
Ex. 3
- Point to j J, k K and l L on the board and let the children look at them and say the sounds. Then, with your back to the class, trace the shapes of the capital letters in the air and let the children copy you, using their forefingers.

- (L1) Tell the children to trace over the letters at the top of the page in their books, using their fingers. Then they can join the dots with their pencils.

- Now teach them the names of the letters: j /dʒeɪ/; k /keɪ/; l /el/. To practise the names of letters, hold up a letter card and ask children to call out the name of the letter. Include all letters learned so far (A–L). You could do this in teams.

- In the second part of the exercise in their books the children must join the small letters to their big friends. Go over the first one, J, with them. Go round and check the children's work.

PB page 17
Ex. 4
- First point to each picture/word on the board. Ask the children *What's this?* They say *a tree*, etc. You may want to rub the pictures/words off the board before the class do the exercise. If the children can read the words, rub them off. If they are likely to have great difficulty with this exercise, leave the pictures/words on the board.

- Now ask the children to look at their books. (L1) Explain that they have to look at the picture, read the words underneath and put a tick in the right box. Do the first example with the class.

Song
- Play the song and join in the words. Let the children listen to it. Play it again and encourage the children to join in. Play it a third time and all sing it together.

    One bird in the tree.
    Two boats on the sea.
    Three kites in the sky.
    Four planes way up high.

Way in B: **Unit 5**

LESSON 1

New language	Known language	
here	Where's . . . ?	a boat
	I'm on the . . .	a chair

Preparation
- Bring in a blindfold (a scarf).

Revision
- (L1) Ask a child to come out and whisper to her or him to put your book on a chair somewhere in the classroom. Go out or close your eyes while this is being done. Come in or open your eyes. Exclaim *Where's the book?* Say it several times. Give the children the opportunity to say *It's on the chair*. If they can't say it then you can find the book and say the sentence. They can repeat it. Now sit on your chair and say *I'm on the chair*. Let the children imitate you and say *I'm on the chair*. Go around the class and whisper to three or four children to remain sitting on their chairs. The rest of the class stands up. Look around and pretend not to see the children on the chairs. Say *Where's (Maria)?* She answers *I'm on the chair*. Do the same with the other children.

**Presentation
PB page 18**
- Pam and Otto are playing 'Hide and Seek'. Pam is looking for Otto. He's under the boat but when Pam's back is turned he is cheeky and stands on the boat waving, knowing Pam cannot see him. (L1) Check the children understand. (L1) Tell the children to look at the top picture. Pretend to be Pam. Say *Where's Otto?* The class repeats this after you, several times. They can now look at the bottom picture. Pretend to be Otto, and say *I'm on the boat*. Let the children repeat this a few times.

Practice
- Divide the class into two groups, A and B. Tell group A that they are Pam and group B that they are Otto. Group A repeats after you *Where's Otto?* Group B repeats after you *I'm on the boat*.

- Now divide the class up into their usual smaller groups. Let group 1 ask *Where's Otto?* Group 2 replies *I'm on the boat*. Then group 2 asks the question and group 3 replies, etc.

- (L1) Ask if any two children want to come out and be Pam and Otto. You can put Otto under and then on a table and he can say instead *I'm on the table*.

Activity
- Find an open area in the classroom or take the class out into the playground. Blindfold two children, 'Otto' and his 'mother' or 'father'. (L1) Explain further that 'father/mother' says *Otto, where are you?* Otto replies *Here*. Mother/father tries to catch Otto – but Otto tries to avoid being caught. When Otto is caught select two more children to be 'mother/father' and 'Otto'.

LESSON 2	New language	Known language
	I'm under . . .	I'm . . .
		in
		the boat

Preparation
- Bring in a large box (large enough to hold a child).
- Make flashcards for 'I'm under the table', 'I'm on the chair' and 'I'm in the box'.

Revision
- Show the children the box and put a pencil in it. Give them the opportunity to say *It's in the box*. If they cannot say it then say the sentence for them and they repeat it.

Presentation
- Put the pencil under the box and say *It's under the box*. Say it several times. Let the children repeat it. Divide the class quickly into their small groups and they repeat it after you. Get under a chair and say *I'm under the chair*. Say it a few times. Let the children get under their chairs and say *I'm under the chair*. Group 1 can say it, then group 2, etc.

PB page 19
- Pam still can't find Otto. He's hiding under the boat again. Belinda plays a joke and turns the boat up. It makes Otto dizzy. (L1) Check that the class understand the story.

- (L1) Tell the class to look at Otto. He is saying that he is under the boat. Pretend to be Otto, and say *I'm under the boat*. Let the class repeat it after you several times. Now, looking at the bottom picture, say *I'm in the boat*. The children repeat this a few times.

Practice
- Divide the class up into their usual groups. Tell them that they are Otto. They must look at the pictures while saying the sentence. Say *I'm under the boat*. Group 1 repeats it, group 2, and so on. Next say *I'm in the boat*. Group 2 repeats it, then group 3, etc.

- (L1) Ask if three children would like to come out and act or mime the whole story.

PB page 20 Ex. 1
- Sit on your chair, hold the flashcard 'I'm on the chair' and say the sentence. Let the children sit on their chairs, look at the card and say *I'm on the chair*. They can say it several times. Get under the table and say *I'm under the table*. Show the children the flashcard 'I'm under the table.' (They might have to gather round you for this!) Put as many children as you can under the table and let them say *I'm under the table*. Show them all the flashcard and they look and read it. Next climb into the box. Stand there and say *I'm in the box*. Show the children the flashcard and say the sentence. Get out and put some children in the box. They say *I'm in the box*. Show them the flashcard and they look and say *I'm in the box*.

- (L1) Explain the exercise. They look at the pictures and read the two sentences. One only is right and they must put a tick in the correct box. (L1) Tell the class to look at the first picture, Tubs. Read both sentences to the children. They read them after you. Ask which one is right. They all put a tick in the first box. Go through each picture, reading both sentences. Let the children read them and ask them where to put the tick. Let them do the last one on their own.

Song • Let the class listen to the song that they will learn in the next lesson.

LESSON 3

New language	Known language	
a mouse	an octopus	
a nose	nine	

Preparation
- Write m M, n N, o O on the board.
- Prepare flashcards for 'mouse', 'nose', 'octopus' and 'nine'.
- Draw a mouse, a nose, an octopus and the numeral 9 on the board and label them.

PB page 21
Ex. 2
- Point to the letters m M, n N, o O on the board. Ask the children to say their sounds. Then with your back to the class, trace the capital letters in the air, saying the sound at the same time. The children copy each one after you, using their forefingers.
- (L1) Tell the children to trace over the letters at the top of the page with their fingers. Then they can join the dots with their pencils. Check their posture and ensure that they are holding their pencils correctly and that their books are straight.
- Now point to each letter on the board and say its sound and then its name. Let the children repeat the sound and the name after you. (L1) Tell them that you will say a name and a volunteer can come up and point to the right letter on the board. Do this a few times.
- Now ask the children to do the second part of the exercise in their books. They have to look at the small letter outside the circle and find a big letter that matches it inside the circle. Go over 'o' with the class. Go around and check that they are doing the task correctly. Ask individual children to tell you the names of the letters.

PB page 21
Ex. 3
- Point to each picture on the board and ask *What's this?* The children say *a mouse, an octopus, nine*. Point to your nose and say *What's this?* They answer *a nose*. Point to the mouse, say *mouse* and hold up the flashcard. The children look at the card and say *mouse* a few times. Point to your nose, say *nose* and hold up the flashcard and repeat it. The children look at the flashcard and say *nose* a few times. Point to the picture of the octopus. Say *octopus*. Hold up the flashcard 'octopus' and say it. Let the class look at the card and say *octopus* a few times. Hold up nine fingers and count to nine. The children count after you. Point to the numeral, say *nine* and hold up the flashcard. Say *nine* again. Let the children look at the flashcard and say *nine*.
- (L1) Ask for volunteers to come out and match the flashcards to the pictures/words. Then rub out the words and ask for four children to come out and match them again.

● Now tell the children to look at exercise 3 in their books. (L1) Explain that they have to look at the two pictures, read the word and decide what picture matches the word. Do the first example with the class. Go around and help the slower children.

Song and rhyme

● Play the rhyme and join in with the words. Play it again and encourage the children to join in. Play it a third time, and all say it together.

A, B, C, D, E, F, G,
H, I, J, K, L, M,
N, O, P, Q,
R, S, T, U,
V, W, X, Y, Z.
G is for green.
H is for head.
I is for ice cream.
J is for jump.
K is for kite.
L is for like.
M is for mouse.
N is for nose.
O is for Otto.
P is for Pam.

Way in B: **Unit 6**

LESSON 1

New language	Known language
take	I'm . . .
big	
little	
steps	

Preparation
- Prepare a big book and a small book; a big ruler and a small ruler; a big chair and a small chair.
- Make flashcards for 'I'm big', 'I'm little'.

Presentation
- (L1) Ask the children what big animals they know. What little ones do they know? Hold up a big book and say *big*. Hold up a small book and say *little*. Have one in each hand. Hold up the big book and say *big* again and then the small book and say *little*. Do it again and let the children repeat it after you. (L1) Check that they understand. Bring a child out in front of the class. Point to yourself and say *big* and point to the child and say *little*. Do it again and let the class repeat it after you. They can repeat it in their groups; group 1 first, then group 2, etc.
- Play 'Jumping the line'. Draw a line in chalk on the classroom floor. (L1) Remind the class that they have played this game before. You say a word and hold up an object. If it is true then they all jump to the 'true' side, but if it is false, i.e. if the word and the object don't match, they all jump to the 'false' side. Hold up a big book and say *big*. They jump to the 'true' side. Hold up a small ruler and say *big*. They jump to the 'false' side. Play this for a few minutes.

PB page 22
- Belinda is saying that she is big. Tubs is saying he is little. (L1) Check that the class understand. (L1) Tell them to look at Belinda. Pretend to be her and say *I'm big*. Say it a few times. Let the class repeat *I'm big* after you. Looking at the bottom picture, pretend to be Tubs and say *I'm little*. Say it several times and the children repeat it.

Practice
- Divide the class up into their groups. (L1) Tell them to pretend to be Belinda and Tubs. Say *I'm big*. Group 1 repeats it after you, then group 2, and so on. Pretend to be Tubs and say *I'm little*. Let group 2 repeat it, group 3, etc.
- (L1) Ask if any of the class wishes to come out and pretend to be Belinda or Tubs and say the sentence.
- Ask the children if they think they are big or little. Compared to grown ups they are little! Tell them to say *I'm little*.

Activities
- Take the children out into the playground or use an open area in the classroom. (L1) Explain the word 'step' by taking a step and saying *one step*, then taking two steps and saying *two steps*. You sit on a chair and the class stands behind a line at some distance from you. Give instructions to individual players telling them to move forward, e.g. *Take five little steps Maria and Anna. Take two big steps Jo and Peter.* Give these instructions to a lot of pupils so that the whole class are involved. The

93

children move forwards as directed. If you think a player has cheated by taking steps that are too large shout *Go back!* and they must go back to the beginning. When a player gets near you he or she can touch you. (The player decides when to touch you.) You must try and catch this player before he or she runs back 'home', i.e. behind the line.

● Point to yourself and say *I'm big*. Show the flashcard 'I'm big' and say it. Let the class look at the card and say *I'm big*. Ask a child to come out and whisper in her or his ear *I'm little*. The child repeats it aloud. Hold up the card 'I'm little' and say the sentence. Let the children look at it and read it after you a few times. If there are pictures of Belinda and Tubs up on the classroom wall you could put the 'I'm big' flashcard next to the elephant's picture and the 'I'm little' flashcard next to the turtle's.

LESSON 2

New language	Known language
	big
	little
	It's . . .

Preparation
● Have ready two books (one big, one little), two chairs (one big, one little), two rulers (one big, one little).

Revision
● (L1) Tell the children that you are going to hold up some big things and some little things and you will say *big* or *little*. If it is true, i.e. if you say *big* and the book is big, then they repeat *big*. If it is not true, i.e. if the book is big and you say *little*, then they are silent. Do this quickly.

Presentation
● Point to the big book and say *It's big*. Point to the small book and say *It's little*. (L1) Check that the children understand. Do it again and let the class repeat it after you each time.

PB page 23
● Drago and Otto notice a very big ship. Otto waves. Then all the friends get into a small boat. Tubs is squashed. (L1) Check that the children understand the two scenes.

● (L1) Tell the class to look at the top picture. Pretend to be Drago and say *It's big*. Say it a few times and let the class repeat it each time. (L1) Check that they understand. Tell them to look at the bottom picture. Pretend to be Otto and say *It's little*. Say it a few times and let the class repeat it after you.

Practice
● Divide the class up into their usual groups. They must look at the right pictures as they say these sentences. (L1) Tell them to look at the ship. Pretend to be Drago. Say *It's big*. Group 1 repeats it, then group 2, and so on. They must look at the bottom picture. Pretend to be Otto and say *It's little*. Group 2 repeats it, group 3, and so on.

● (L1) Ask if five children want to come out and act the scenes. They can pretend to cram themselves into a tiny boat.

- Point to the big chair and say *It's big*. Show the children the flashcard 'It's big'. Say it and let them look and repeat it after you. Point to the little chair and say *It's little*. Show the flashcard 'It's little' and say the sentence. Let the children look and repeat it after you. Quickly point to yourself, say *I'm big* and show the 'I'm big' flashcard. Say it again and let the children look and repeat it. Whisper in a child's ear *I'm little*. She or he says *I'm little* aloud. Show the 'I'm little' flashcard and say the sentence. Let the children look at it and say it.

- (L1) Tell the class that you will hold up one of the four flashcards. They must look at it, read it and then point to something big or something little or something big (i.e. you) or someone little (i.e. the children themselves). Hold up each flashcard twice and wait for the children to point. All this is done in silence.

**PB page 24
Ex. 1**

- (L1) Explain to the class that they have to look at the pictures, read the sentences and match the pictures to the sentences. Read the four sentences to the children. They read them after you. Go over the first example with the children. Let them do the last three. Go around and help individual children.

**PB page 24
Ex. 2**

- (L1) Ask the children if they are big or little. They are little. (L1) Explain that they can draw themselves in the space and colour it in. Let them do this first.

- Next write 'I'm little' on the board. The children must look carefully at the way you form the letters. Trace the sentence with your back to them with your finger. Say the name of each letter as you do it. The children, using their forefingers, trace each letter in the air after you. They can then trace over the letters on the page with their fingers, and join the dots together using their pencils. Finally they can write the sentence freehand underneath. Check their posture, that their books are straight and that they are holding their pencils correctly. Go around and help individual children form the letters. Ask them to read the sentence to you.

Rhyme

- If there is time let the class listen to the rhyme that they will learn next lesson.

LESSON 3

New language	Known language
	a radio
	a plane

Preparation

- Write p P, q Q, r R on the board.

- Draw a radio, a plane, and Pam on the board and label them.

Revision

- Play this alphabet game to revise the names of the letters the children have learnt so far. Sit the children in a row or rows. (L1) Tell a child to walk up and down the rows and stop behind any child. Write any letter from A to O on the board. The two children shout out the name of the letter. The one to shout the correct name first wins and he or she walks up and down the rows next.

PB page 25
Ex. 3

- Point to p P, q Q and r R on the board and remind the class of their sounds. Then, with your back to the class, trace the shape of each capital letter in the air, saying the sound as you do so. Let the children copy you.

- Ask the children to trace over the letters at the top of page 25 with their fingers and then join the dots with their pencils to form the letters.

- Now teach the names of the letters: p /piː/; q /kjuː/; r /aːr/. Practise the names briefly by continuing the alphabet game above, using only P, Q and R.

- (L1) Ask the children to look at the second part of exercise 3 in their books. Explain that they have to look at the small letter on the left and find the big friend that matches it among the letters on the right. When they have found it they circle it. Go around and check that the children are doing the exercise correctly. Ask individual children to tell you the names and sounds of the letters.

PB page 25
Ex. 4

- Point to each picture/word on the board. Let the children say what each is: *a radio, a plane, Pam.* Rub out the pictures and let the children read the three words aloud. (L1) Tell them that you will point to a word and they can now say it. Do it at random.

- (L1) Explain the exercise to the class. They have to read the word and draw a picture in the space provided. The picture will be one of the ones at the top of the exercise. Do the first one with the class: the radio. Go around while the children are doing this and help those who have problems.

Song

- Play the song on the cassette and join in the words while the children listen to it. Play it again and let the class do the actions and encourage them to say the words. Play it again and everyone joins in and does the actions.

> Belinda walks like this and that. *(Walk like an elephant.)*
> She's very big.
> She's very fat.
> She has no fingers.
> She has no toes.
> But, goodness gracious, what a nose!
> *(Do an imitation of an elephant's trunk.)*

Way in B: **Unit 7**

LESSON 1

New language	Known language
a camera	I have . . .
a trumpet	

Preparation
- Bring in a camera and a trumpet or pictures of them.
- Make a 'lucky dip'. Wrap up objects in paper and put them in a box for the children to pick them out. Choose objects they know the names of.

Revision
- Quickly sing the song from *Way in A*, Unit 7, Lesson 3, 'I have a house'.

  I have a house
  And in my house
  I have a floor
  And a window and a door.

  I have a house
  And in my house
  I have a cat
  And a rabbit and a hat.

Presentation
- Teach the new items. Point to the camera and say *a camera*. Say it several times and let the children repeat it after you. Next point to the trumpet (or a picture of one) and say *a trumpet*. Say it a few times and let the children repeat it after you. Put the camera in one hand and the trumpet in the other. The children have to listen to you and then point to the object you name. Say *I have a trumpet*. The children point. Say *I have a camera*. The class points. Do this a few times.

PB page 26
- (L1) Ask the children if they have ever seen a 'lucky dip' where they put in a hand and pull out a surprise present. Here Pam has pulled out a camera and Belinda and Otto are putting in a trunk and tentacles. Otto is cheating! Belinda gets a trumpet. (L1) Check that the class understand the situation.
- Looking at the top picture pretend to be Pam and say *I have a camera*. Say it a few times. Let the children repeat it after you. Now while looking at the bottom picture pretend to be Belinda. Say *I have a trumpet*. Say it several times. Let the children repeat it after you.

Practice
- Divide the children up into their usual groups. Tell them to look at Pam and say *I have a camera*. Group 1 repeats it, then group 2, etc. Next, they are Belinda, say *I have a trumpet*. Group 2 repeats it, group 3, and so on.
- (L1) Ask if any of them want to come out and be Pam and Belinda.

Activity
- Put the 'lucky dip' at the front of the class and gather the children around it. (L1) Explain that they must pick out a parcel, feel it, and guess what it is first. Then they open it and say, *I have a (hat)*. The children can do this in turns. Make sure you have a parcel for every child.

LESSON 2

New language	Known language
I have a . . . and a . . .	I have . . .
a guitar	
a drum	

Preparation
- Bring in a guitar, a drum, a trumpet, and a camera or pictures of them.

Presentation
- Teach the new items. Hold up, or point to the picture of, a guitar. Say *a guitar* several times. The children repeat it after you. (L1) Ask them if they know anyone who plays a guitar. Who? Now hold up the drum. Say *a drum*. Say it several times. Let the children repeat it after you. (L1) Ask if any of them play the drum.

- Now put the four objects, or pictures of them, at the front of the classroom. Divide the class into two teams, A and B. (L1) Quickly explain that you are going to say the name of an object and two players, one from team A and one from team B, must run out and touch the right one. The first to touch it wins a point. Play this for a few minutes only.

PB page 27
- (L1) Ask the class if any of them play a musical instrument. Now do they remember what Otto was doing with the 'lucky dip'? Yes, he was putting in two tentacles. Tell the children (L1) to look at the page and see what happened. Otto picked out a guitar and a drum. (L1) Check that they understand. Pretend to be Otto and say *I have a guitar and a drum*. Say it several times and let the children repeat it after you each time.

Practice
- Divide the class up into their groups. Pretend to be Otto and say *I have a guitar and a drum*. Group 1 repeats it, then group 2, and so on.

PB page 28
Ex. 1
- (L1) Explain to the class that they have to listen to you very carefully. You will say a sentence and if it matches the picture then they put a tick in the box. If the sentence and the picture don't match, then they put a cross in the box.

  1) I have a camera.
  2) I have a cake.
  3) I have a guitar.
  4) I have a drum.

  Say the sentences a few times to give the children the opportunity to get the answers right. Go around and check their work.

PB page 28
Ex. 2
- (L1) Ask the children what Drago has got. What is he saying? They answer *I have a guitar*. Write the sentence on the board and let the children look carefully at how you form the letters. Trace the sentence in the air with your back to the class. Say each letter as you do so. Let the children trace the letters using their forefingers, imitating you. (L1) Tell them to trace over the sentence on the page with their forefingers. Then they can join the dots together. Finally they can write the sentence freehand. Remind them to sit properly, hold their pencils correctly and keep their books

straight. Go around and help individual children write the letters. They can read the sentence to you.

Song
- If there is time let the children listen to the song that they will learn next lesson.

LESSON 3

New language	Known language
	seven
	an umbrella
	a tail

Preparation
- Draw a picture of a tail, an umbrella and the numerals 5, 6 and 7 on the board.
- Write s S, t T, u U on the board at the children's height.

PB page 29
Ex. 3
- Point to s S, t T and u U on the board and ask the children to say what sounds the letters make. Then, with your back to the class, trace the shapes of the letters in the air and ask the children to copy you, saying the sounds of the letters at the same time.
- Now the children go over the letters in their books, first with their fingers, then with their pencils, joining the dots.
- Now teach the children the names of the letters: s /es/; t /tiː/; u /juː/. Now say the name of one of those letters and ask a volunteer to come to the board and put a ring round the right letter. Do this a few times.
- In the second part of the exercise on page 29 the children have to find the big letter inside the circle which matches the small one outside. They should circle the correct letter and draw a line from it to the small one. Go over the first example with the class.

PB page 29
Ex. 4
- Point to the pictures of a tail, an umbrella and the numerals 6 and 7 on the board and give the children the opportunity to say what each one is. Write the word when they say it underneath. Say each word again and they repeat it while looking at it. Rub the pictures and words off the board.
- Explain to the class that they now have to look at the pictures, read the words and draw a line from the picture to the word that matches. Go over the first example with the children: 'umbrella'.

Song
- Play the song for the children to listen to while you join in the words. Play it again and encourage them to join in. The third time let everyone sing the words. The children can pretend to have a drum and bang it, and a flute and 'toot' it.

  1 I have a drum,
     A big, big drum.
     Dr – um, dr – um,
     Listen to my drum.

2   I have a flute,
     A small, small flute.
     Toot, toot,
     Listen to my flute.

3   I have a drum,
     A big, big drum.
     Dr – um, dr – um,
     Listen to my drum.

Way in B: **Unit 8**

LESSON 1

New language	Known language
Is it a . . . ?	a cake
No.	

Preparation
- Bring in a cake and a drum or pictures of them. Label them.

Presentation
- Draw part of a table on the board. Before you complete it, stand back from it and say *Is it a chair?* Then answer yourself, say *No.* Pretend to look puzzled again and say *Is it a book?* Then answer *No* and shake your head. Turn to the class and say *What's this?* Give them the opportunity to guess, *a table.* (L1) Explain the question *Is it a . . . ?* and *yes* and *no.* Play the game again. You can play it in other lessons too.

PB page 30
- Tubs is interested in Otto's drum but he doesn't know what it is. He asks *Is it a cake?* and tries to eat it. Otto thinks this very funny. (L1) Check that the children understand the situation. (L1) Tell them to look at the top picture. Pretend to be Tubs and say *Is it a cake?* Say it a few times. Let the children repeat it after you. Pretend to be Otto and say *No.* Again say it a few times and let the children repeat it.

Practice
- First divide the class into two large groups, A and B. (L1) Tell group A they are Tubs and group B that they are Otto. Pretend to be Tubs and say *Is it a cake?* Group A repeat it. Say *No* and group B repeat it. Change the groups around. Let group B ask Tubs' question and group A answer.

- Now divide the class into their usual groups. Group 1 asks the question, group 2 replies, then group 2 asks and group 3 replies, and so on. Each group has an opportunity to ask and answer.

- (L1) Ask if any two children want to come out and be Otto and Tubs.

Activity
- Play the game *Is it a . . . ?* from the beginning of the lesson, but first draw an incomplete object and the children individually ask *Is it a . . . ?* Choose objects that they know the English for, e.g. mouse, bread, box, parts of the body, etc. Give every child the opportunity to have a turn.

LESSON 2

New language	Known language
Yes.	Is it a . . . ?
	a drum

Preparation
- Wrap up some objects in parcels, e.g. a book, an apple, a hat (the children must know their names in English).

Revision
- Hold up a wrapped parcel, feel it and say *Is it an egg?* Pass it around the class and individual children say *Is it a (book)?* Each child has to guess a different object and

then pass it on. After four or five guesses a child can open it and show what it is, e.g. a box.

Presentation

- Pam is asking if it is a drum. She taps it. Yes says Otto and hits it very hard to show it is a drum. Pam and Tubs have sore ears! (L1) Tell the class to look at the top picture. Pretend to be Pam and say *Is it a drum?* Say it a few times and let the children look at the picture and say it after you each time. Now they can look at Otto banging his drum. (L1) Explain that he is saying *Yes*. Pretend to be Otto. Say *Yes*. Say it a few times. Let the class repeat it.

Practice

- Divide the class into two large groups, A and B. (L1) Tell group A they are Pam and group B they are Otto. Ask the question *Is it a drum?* Group A repeats it. You reply *Yes*. Group B repeats it. Do this a few times. Change the groups around so that group B is Pam and asks the question and group A is Otto and replies. Now divide the class up into their usual smaller groups. Let group 1 ask the question while looking at the picture, *Is it a drum?* and group 2 looks and replies *Yes*. Then group 2 asks and group 3 answers, etc. Continue until each group has asked and answered the question.

- (L1) Ask if three children would like to come out and act out the whole story.

PB page 32 Ex. 1

- Play 'Word Bingo'. The children have played this game with letters and numbers in *Way in A*. (L1) Remind them of the rules. Divide them into six groups. Each group has a card with six words on the card. Give each group six pieces of small plain paper each so that they can cover up the words. You will take out a flashcard from the bag and hold it up. If a group has that word then they put up their hands and say the word. They must be able to show you the word on their card. If they have the word and can say it then that group can cover over the word with the piece of paper. The first group to have all six words covered is the winner.

- You may like to change the groups around after one game so that the children have the opportunity to learn to read all the words.

Rhyme

- If there is time let the children listen to the rhyme that they will learn next lesson.

LESSON 3

New language	Known language	
	box	six
	window	seven

Preparation

- Bring in a box.

- Draw the numerals 6 and 7 on the board.

- Write v V, w W, x X on the board.

**PB page 33
Ex. 2**

- Point to the letters v V, w W and x X on the board and ask the class what sounds those letters make. Then trace the shapes of the capital letters in the air, with your back to the class, and let them copy you.

- Then ask the children to trace over the letters at the top of the page with their fingers, and finally to join the dots using their pencils.

- Now teach the names of the letters: v /viː/; w /dʌbəljuː/; x /eks/. Let the children look and repeat the names after you. Do this a few times. (L1) Tell the class that you are going to point to a letter and say its name. If it is correct they put up one hand; if it is wrong they put up both hands. Play this very quickly.

- In the second part of the exercise the children have to look at the small letter on the left and find its big friend among the letters on the right. Go around and help individual children.

**PB page 33
Ex. 3**

- Point to the window and say *What's that?* Give the class the opportunity to answer *a window*. Write 'window' on the board. Point to it and say it. Let the children look and say it. Now hold up the box. Let the children say *a box*. Write 'box' on the board. Say it and let the class look and say it. Point to '6' and they say *six*. Write 'six' on the board, say it and let the children look and say. Point to '7' and the class say *seven*. Write 'seven' and say it. The children look and say *seven*.

- (L1) Remind the class how to do crosswords. Tell them to fill the four words in. Go around and help individual children.

Rhyme

- Play the rhyme for the class and join in the words. Play it again and encourage them to join in. Play it a third time.

> Give me a D,
> Give me an R,
> Give me an A,
> Give me a G,
> Give me an O.
> DRAGO!

LESSON 1

New language	Known language	
That's my . . .	That's . . .	a book
a house	a boat	a chair

Preparation

- Draw a house and a boat on the board.

- Prepare two flashcards, 'That's my house.', 'That's my boat.'.

Presentation

- Point to a book (not yours) and say *That's a book*. The children look at the book and repeat the sentence after you. Point to your book (and make sure the class know it's your book) and say *That's my book*. Say it a few times. They do not repeat the sentence after you. Point to your chair and say *That's my chair*. Say it several times. (L1) Check that the children understand the sentence. (L1) Tell them to point to their own books and say *That's my book* a few times. Now they can stand and point to their chairs and say, *That's my chair*. They repeat it several times. Indicate the picture of a house on the board and say *a house*. Let the children repeat it.

PB page 34

- Pam is taking Drago to show him her house and her things. (L1) Check that the children understand that Pam is telling Drago that it is her house. (L1) Pretend to be Pam and tell the class to look at the first picture. Say *That's my house* a few times. Now the children pretend to be Pam and repeat the sentence after you while looking at the picture. (L1) Tell them to look at the bottom picture. Say *That's my boat* a few times. The children repeat it after you.

Practice

- (L1) Remind the children to look at the pictures while they say the sentence. Divide the class up into their usual groups. They are all pretending to be Pam. Say *That's my house*. Group 1 repeats it after you, group 2, and so on. Next say *That's my boat*. Let group 2 repeat it, then group 3, and so on.

- (L1) Ask if any two children want to come out and be Pam and Drago. 'Pam' can point to the pictures on the board at the appropriate time.

Activities

- (L1) Tell the children to draw a boat in their exercise books. Say *Draw a boat*. Then go around and encourage the children to point to it and say *That's my boat*. You may like to write the sentence for them underneath when they have said it.

- Quickly draw another house on the board. Point to it and say *That's my house*. Show the flashcard 'That's my house', say it and let the children look at it and say it. Draw another boat quickly on the board. Say *That's my boat* and hold up the flashcard. Say *That's my boat* and the children look and repeat it. (L1) Ask for two volunteers to come up and match the right sentence to the right picture. If they have difficulty write the sentences underneath the pictures and ask them to try again.

- If there is time you may like to play 'Jumping the line' with the class. Draw a line; one side is true, the other false. You point to the house and show the flashcard 'That's my house'. It's true, so the children jump to the true side. If you show 'That's my boat' and point to the house, then they jump to the false side.

LESSON 2	**New language** a bike	**Known language** That's my . . . a head

Preparation

- Draw a bike on the board.

Presentation

- Point to the bike on the board and say *a bike*. Say it a few times. Let the class repeat it after you. (L1) Ask who has a bike.

PB page 35

- Pam has been showing Drago around her place. Now Drago is riding her bike and Pam is worried. He is going straight towards a tree. Drago crashes and Pam takes his photo. (L1) Check that the children understand. Tell them that they are going to be Pam and to look at the top picture. Say *That's my bike*. Say it a few times and let the children look at the picture and repeat it. Pretend to be Drago. Hold your head and say *Oh, my head*. (L1) Check that they understand. Say it again. Let the children hold their heads, like Drago, and say *Oh, my head* several times.

Practice

- Divide the class up into two groups, A and B. (L1) Tell group A that they are Pam and group B that they are Drago. Say *That's my bike* and group A looks at the picture and repeats it. Say *Oh, my head* while holding your head and group B repeats it. They must look at the picture and hold their heads. Change the groups around so group A is Drago and group B is Pam. Let them say the sentences.

- Divide the class into their usual smaller groups. Group 1 says both sentences, then group 2, and so on. Make sure that they are looking at the pictures while they say the sentences.

- (L1) Ask if two children would like to come out and act the whole story.

PB page 36
Ex. 1

- (L1) Explain to the class that they have to look at the picture and read the two sentences. One sentence is right. They have to put a tick in the box opposite the right sentence. (L1) Ask the children to look at Drago. What is he pointing at? Read the two sentences aloud to the class, and they read them after you. Which is right? *That's my mouse*. They must therefore put the tick in the top box. Do the same with each picture and sentences. You read them, then the children read them. Go around and make sure that they have ticked the right box. Finally, read out the three correct sentences and let the children read them after you.

PB page 36
Ex. 2

- (L1) Explain to the class that Pam is pointing to her house. Ask what they think she is saying. Yes, *That's my house*. Read the sentence aloud and the children look at the sentence and read it. Write the sentence on the board and say the words as you do so. Trace the sentence in the air with your back to the class.

- The children, using their forefingers, trace over the letters on the page first, then they can trace over the dots with their pencils. (L1) Remind them to hold their pencils correctly, to sit properly and to put their books straight in front of them. Finally, they can write the sentence freehand. Go around and check their work, helping individual children to form the letters. Read the sentence to each of them and they look at it and repeat it after you. (L1) Check that they understand it.

Song
- If there is time let the children listen to the song that they will learn in the next lesson.

LESSON 3

New language	Known language

Preparation
- Write y Y, z Z on the board.

PB page 37 Ex. 3
- Point to y Y and z Z on the board and tell the children that these are the last letters of the alphabet. With your back to the class trace the shapes of the capital letters in the air and let the class copy you, using their forefingers. Say the sounds of the letters as you do so.

- Now let the children trace over the letters at the top of the page with their fingers and then join the dots with their pencils.

- Say the names of the letters, y /waɪ/ and z /zed/ and let the children repeat them after you a few times.

- In the second part of the exercise the children must look in the circle and find the big letter that matches the small letter outside the circle. They put a ring round the big letter and draw a line joining it to the small one.

PB page 37 Ex. 4
- Quickly write up half of the alphabet on the board, A–M. Make sure they are at the children's height. Say the names of the letters as you do so. Let the class say them after you.

- (L1) Ask for volunteers to come out and join the letters on the board in sequence A—B—C etc. (L1) Explain to the children that in the exercise at the bottom of the page they have to join the letters together in the right order. When they are doing it go around and help those who are slower. Let them tell you the names of the letters.

Song and rhyme
- Play the rhyme through first while the children listen. Play it a second time and let the children join in where they can. Play it a third time and all say the words together all the way through.

A, B, C, D, E, F, G,
H, I, J, K, L, M,
N, O, P, Q,
R, S, T, U,
V, W, X, Y, Z.
Q is for queen.
R is for red.

S is for sea.
T is for tree.
U is for umbrella.
V is for van.
W is for white.
X is for X-ray.
Y is for you.
And Z is for zoo.

Further suggestions

● You may like to play Bingo with capital letters and using letter names at this point. Make twenty-six letter cards and put capital letters on each one. Then either make Bingo cards with six different letters on each of them or write 'cards' with the letters on them on the board and give each group a different set of letters. Play it in the usual way.

● To revise the names of the letters of the alphabet you could play 'Winner says M' from *Bonanza*.

Way in B: **Unit 10**

LESSON 1

New language	Known language
shells	one–ten
flags	

Preparation
- Bring in some shells and flags. Alternatively draw them on the board.
- Make flashcards for 'shells' and 'flags'.

Revision
- Quickly revise numbers 1 to 10 with the class. Knock a number of times and let them tell you how many times you knocked. Do this a few times. Then you say a number from 1 to 10 and they clap that many times.

Presentation
- Show the shells or point to the picture. Say *shells*. Say it a few times. Let the children repeat it after you. Now show them the flags. Say *flags* a few times. Let the children repeat it after you. Put the shells in one hand and the flags in the other. (L1) Tell the class that you will say a word and they have to point to the hand holding that object. Do this quickly.

PB page 38
- (L1) Ask the class if they ever make sandcastles on the beach. Otto and Belinda are making a sandcastle. Otto is decorating it, first with shells, then with flags. Belinda is digging a moat around to put water in it. (L1) Check that the class understands and ask what each animal is doing. Count the shells, *One, two, three, four, five. Five shells*. Let the children count after you. Do this a few times. Now they can look at the flags. Count *One, two, three, four, five, six. Six flags*. Let the children count after you. Do this several times.

Practice
- Divide the class into their usual groups. Remind them to look at the pictures as they say the words. Looking at the top picture say *Five shells*. Group 1 repeats it after you, group 2, and so on. Then say *Six flags*. Group 2 looks at the flags and repeats *Six flags*, then group 3, and so on.
- (L1) Ask if any two children would like to come out and pretend to be Otto and Belinda making a lovely sandcastle.

Activity
- (L1) Explain to the children that in this game they have to think of as many classroom objects as possible beginning with a given letter of the alphabet. Divide the class into two teams. You say a letter, e.g. *B*. The first player might say *book*. If any other player can see another object beginning with the letter B, he or she says, for example, *book and box*. If no other player says a word beginning with B after 10 seconds, the second player wins a point for his or her team. The winning team is the first team to win 3 points. You may like to draw various objects on the board to help the game along, e.g. a cat, a boat, a shell, a flag, etc.

LESSON 2	New language	Known language
	stars	flags
		shells
		lemons
		one–ten

Preparation
- Draw five stars, six shells, seven flags and six lemons on the board. Label them 'stars', 'shells', etc. Make flashcards for all four words.

Revision
- Point to the shells and give the class the opportunity to tell you what they are. Point to the flags and the lemons and do the same. (L1) Tell them that you will say a word and point to a picture. If it is right they repeat it. If it is not right they must remain silent. Play the game using shells, flags and lemons only.

Presentation
- Point to the stars and say *stars*. Say it a few times. Let the children say it after you.

PB page 39
- Otto and Belinda are finishing off their sandcastle. They have put seven stars on it and now they are pouring water into the moat. Disaster happens when a wave destroys the sandcastle. (L1) Check that the class understands the situation. How many stars are there? (L1) Tell the class to look at the top picture and count. You count with them. Count aloud again with the class. Say *Seven stars* and let the children repeat it. Do this a few times.

Practice
- Divide the class up into their usual groups. (L1) Remind them to look at the picture. Say *Seven stars*. Group 1 repeats it, then group 2, etc.

- (L1) Ask the children if two of them would like to come out and act out the story.

Activity
- (L1) Tell the children to count the shells, etc. on the board. Give them time to count silently. Now they can say the number of each and what they are, e.g. *Five stars*. Help them with this if they have difficulty. Go through each set with them.

- Point to each group of objects and (L1) ask if any child can come up and match the flashcards to the pictures/words. Encourage them to say *Seven flags*, etc., when they do so. Now rub off the words underneath the pictures and ask if volunteers can come up and match the flashcards to the pictures.

**PB page 40
Ex. 1**
- (L1) Explain to the children that they have to look at the pictures and read the words. Then they draw a line from the right word to the right picture. Go over the first one, 'stars', with them. Go around and praise those who are doing it correctly. Help individual children who have problems.

**PB page 40
Ex. 2**
- (L1) Explain to the class that they must listen carefully. You will say a number and objects. Then they must draw the right number of objects in the circle. Say:

  1) Five doors.
  2) Six lemons.
  3) Seven stars.

Say the sentences several times. Go around the class and check that they are drawing correctly.

- When they have finished, (L1) tell the children to write the numeral and the name of the objects underneath, i.e. 5 doors, 6 lemons, 7 stars. Help the slower children.

Song
- If there is time play the song that the children will learn in the next lesson.

LESSON 3

New language	Known language	
	one–ten	a bike
	a guitar	a house
	a trumpet	

Preparation
- Draw a guitar, a trumpet, a bike, a house on the board and write the words underneath.

- Write the numbers 1–10 at the children's height at random on the board.

- Bring in the twenty-six letter cards.

PB page 41
Ex. 3
- (L1) Ask for volunteers to come out and join the numbers on the board in sequence, 1–2; 2–3; etc. As they join them encourage the children to say the numbers.

- (L1) Explain to the class that they have to join the numbers in the exercise in the right order to make something. When they have completed both pictures they can colour them in. Finally they must write what it is underneath (a star, a flag). Go around and help individual children.

PB page 41
Ex. 4
- Point to the pictures/words on the board and give the children the opportunity to say what they are. Now give out the letter cards quickly. If the class is small give a few cards to each child. (L1) Tell them that you are going to point to a word and children with letters in that word must run out and stand in a line in front of the class, in the right order. For example, point to 'bike'. The children with 'b', 'i', 'k' and 'e' run out and stand facing the class, holding up their letters, so that the rest of the class can see 'bike'. They say *bike*. Do the same with the other three words. Collect the cards.

- (L1) Now ask the children to look at their books and explain that in the tree are four hidden objects. They have to try and find them. When they have found the missing objects they fill in the words underneath with the right letters. Do the first one with the class, 'guitar'. Go around and help individual children. Finally go over the exercise with the class.

Song
- Play the song through first, joining in the words while the children listen. Play it again and encourage them to join in. Play it a third time and all sing it together. The children can hold up the number of fingers as they sing the words.

1   One, two, three,
    On my knee,
    Three little birds.
    Cheep, cheep, cheep.

2   Four, five, six,
    On the sticks,
    Six little birds.
    Cheep, cheep, cheep,
    Cheep, cheep, cheep.

3   Seven, eight, nine,
    On the line,
    Nine little birds.
    Cheep, cheep, cheep,
    Cheep, cheep, cheep.
    Cheep, cheep, cheep.

Way in B: **Unit 11**

LESSON 1

New language	Known language
father	That's my . . .
sister	

Preparation

- Make flashcards for 'father' and 'sister'.

- Draw a man and a young girl on the board. Write 'father' and 'sister' underneath.

PB page 42

- Pam is now showing Drago her family. Her father is windsurfing, her sister is doing handstands on the beach. (L1) Ask the children what Drago is doing. Do they think he will take good photographs? (L1) Check that they understand the situation. (L1) Tell the class to look at the man, and explain that he is Pam's father. Say *father* a few times. The children repeat it. Pretend to be Pam, say *That's my father*. Say it several times. Let the children repeat it. Looking at the bottom picture, explain that this is Pam's sister. Say *sister* a few times. Let the class repeat it after you. Now pretend to be Pam and say *That's my sister*. Say it several times and let the children repeat it after you.

Practice

- Divide the class up into their usual groups. (L1) Remind them to look at each picture as they say the sentences. Everyone pretends to be Pam. Say *That's my father*. The children look and group 1 repeats the sentence, then group 2, and so on. Looking at the bottom picture say *That's my sister*. Group 2 looks and repeats the sentence, then the other groups in turn.

- (L1) Ask if two children want to come out and be Pam and Drago, and two others can come out and be Pam's father and sister.

Activities

- (L1) Tell the children to look at the picture of Pam's father. Say *father* and hold up the flashcard 'father'. They look and say *father*. (L1) Tell them to look at Pam's sister. Say *sister*. Show them the flashcard 'sister'. Say it and the children look and say *sister*. (L1) Ask for volunteers to come up and match the flashcard to the right picture/word. Rub the words off and ask for more volunteers.

- The children can draw a picture of either their father or their sister at this point.

- (L1) Ask the children to bring in photos of their father, mother, brothers and sisters next lesson.

LESSON 2

New language	Known language
brother	That's my . . .
mother	father
	sister

Preparation

- Draw on the board a picture of a young boy and young girl, a man, and a woman. Label them 'My brother', 'My sister', 'My father', 'My mother'.

● Bring in photographs of your family.

Revision
● Hold up a photograph of your father and say *That's my father.* Hold up a photograph of your sister and say *That's my sister.* (Alternatively, draw pictures of them on the blackboard.) Encourage individual children to come out and hold up their photographs and say *That's my father* and *That's my sister.* Make sure there is only one person in each photo!

Presentation
● Hold up a photograph of your brother and say *That's my brother.* Say it a few times. Each child can hold up the photographs, point to them and say *That's my brother.* Let them say it a few times. Then hold up a photograph of your mother, point to it and say *That's my mother.* Say it several times. Let the children hold up their photographs of their mother and say *That's my mother.*

PB page 43
● Pam's brother appears in diving gear. Drago is puzzled. Then Pam shows Drago her mother buried in sand. (L1) Check that the children understand the situations. (L1) Ask what Pam's brother has been doing and who is under the sand. (L1) Tell the children to look at the top picture and pretend to be Pam. Say *That's my brother.* Let the children repeat it a few times. Then they look at the bottom picture and say *That's my mother.* They repeat this several times.

Practice
● Divide the class up into their usual groups. (L1) Remind them to look at the pictures when they say the sentences. Everyone pretends to be Pam. Say *That's my brother.* Group 1 repeats this, then the other groups in turn. Looking at the bottom picture say *That's my mother.* Each group in turn repeats this after you.

● (L1) Ask if four children want to come out and be Pam, Drago, Pam's brother and mother.

● (L1) Ask the children to look at the board. Tell them that this is your family. Point to each picture/word and say *my brother, my sister,* etc., and let the class repeat them after you. (L1) Tell them that you are going to say, for example, *my mother,* and volunteers can come up and point to the correct picture.

PB page 44 Ex. 1
● (L1) Explain to the class that here are four circles in which they have to draw their family. They have to read the words underneath each circle and draw the right person in it. Go through it with the class first. (L1) Tell them to look at the first circle. Say *my mother.* They repeat it. The second circle is *my father.* Continue with the others. Let the children draw and colour in the pictures. Go around and ask individual children to tell you who each is. Encourage them to say *That's my . . . .*

Rhyme
● Play the rhyme that the class will learn next lesson.

LESSON 3	**New language**	**Known language**
		That's my . . .
		mother

Preparation
- Write '6   9   X   2' on the board.

PB page 45
Ex. 2
- (L1) Tell the children to look at the four items on the board. One of them does not fit. They should say (L1) X does not fit. Put a ring around it. (L1) Explain that they have to look at each line in this exercise and they must find out what shape is the odd one out.

  Answers: 1   X
  2   A
  3   i
  4   S

  Go around and help individual children. Finally go over the exercise on the board.

PB page 45
Ex. 3
- Here is Belinda with her mother. (L1) Check that the class understand this. Pretend to be Belinda and say *That's my mother*. Let the children repeat it. Write the sentence on the board and say the words as you do so, then, with your back to the class, trace the sentence in the air. Let the children imitate you, using their forefingers. They can say the words at the same time.

- (L1) Tell the class to trace over the shapes in their book using their forefinger. Then they can join up the dots to form the sentence. (L1) Remind them of their posture, etc. Finally they can write the sentence freehand. Go around and help individual children. Ask them to read you the sentence.

Rhyme
- Play the entire rhyme to the children and say the words and do the actions. Play it again and encourage them to join in with the words and the actions. Play it a third time and everyone can say the words and do the actions.

  This is my father, round and fat.
  (Hold up your thumb.)

  This is my mother with children and cat.
  (Hold up your forefinger.)

  This is my sister, straight and tall.
  (Hold up your middle finger.)

  This is my brother, he's happy and small.
  (Hold up your fourth finger.)

  This is the baby, eating his toe.
  (Hold up your little finger.)

  And this is the family, all in a row.
  (Hold up all five fingers.)

Way in B: **Unit 12**

LESSON 1

New language	Known language
This is your . . .	a boat
	a bike

Presentation

- (L1) Explain to the class that you want them to draw two things very quickly in their exercise books. Say *Draw a boat*. Repeat this instruction a few times. Go around and check that they understand. Now say *Draw a bike*. Again repeat this several times and check their work. Choose a child's picture of a boat. Hold it up and say to the child *This is your boat*. Say it a few times. (L1) Check that the children understand the meaning. Say it again and let the rest of the class repeat it (*not* the child whose picture it is!). Pick up another exercise book and show the class. Say to the child *This is your boat*. Let the class repeat it after you. Make sure you praise the pictures that they have drawn. Choose a picture of a bike. Hold it up, show the class, and say to the child *This is your bike*. Say it several times. Let the rest of the class look at the child and say *This is your bike*. Do the same with several other pictures.

PB page 46

- (L1) Remind the class that Drago has been taking photographs but he is not a very good photographer. Both photographs are awful. (L1) Ask the children what they can see in both pictures and check that they understand the situation. (L1) Tell them to look at the top picture. Pretend to be Drago. Say *This is your boat*. (L1) Check that the children realize it's Pam's boat but that she is puzzled. Say it again and let the class repeat it after you several times. Looking at the bottom picture say *This is your bike*. (L1) Check that the children understand. Say it again and let the class repeat it after you a few times.

Practice

- Divide the class into their usual groups. Remind them to look at the pictures while they say the sentences. Everyone pretends to be Drago. Say *This is your boat*. Group 1 repeats it, then group 2, etc. Say *This is your bike*. Group 2 repeats it, group 3, etc.

- (L1) Ask if two children would like to come out and pretend to be Pam and Drago. They could use their drawings for the boat and the bike.

Activities

- (L1) Ask for four volunteers to come out and draw some objects. Then give a different instruction to each child.

  1) Draw a cake.
  2) Draw an egg.
  3) Draw a drum.
  4) Draw a book.

  Praise them for their drawings. Then point to each picture and look at the artist and say *This is your (cake)*. When you say the sentence write it under each picture and say it. Let the class repeat it after you.

- Play 'Drago says' (L1) Remind the class of the game; every time you give an instruction they must only obey if you start off with the words 'Drago says . . .'. If they do the action when you don't say 'Drago says . . .' then they are out. Include

115

instructions such as *swim, fly* and the children can mime the actions. You can also say *jump, run, draw*, as well as *Touch your (head, ear, leg, etc.).*

● (L1) Remind the children to bring in a photograph of their whole family next lesson.

LESSON 2

New language	Known language
This is your . . .	
family	

Preparation
● Bring in a photograph of your family.

Presentation
● Hold up a photograph of your family. Point to each person and say *mother, father,* etc. Gesture that altogether they make *a family.* (L1) Check that the children understand *a family.* Say *a family* a few times and let them repeat it after you. Choose a child's photograph and say to the child *This is your family.* Say it a few times. Get the rest of the class to look at the child and say the sentence. Do the same with a few other photographs.

PB page 47
● Drago has taken a photograph of Pam's family but heads and feet are muddled up. Pam is very angry with Drago. (L1) Ask the children what they can see in the top picture. (L1) Tell them to look at the photograph and pretend to be Drago. Say *This is your family.* (L1) Check that the class understands. Say it several times and let the children repeat it after you. Looking at the second picture pretend to be Drago and make an *Ouch!* sound. Let the class imitate you.

Practice
● Divide the class into their usual groups. Everyone pretends to be Drago. (L1) Remind the children to look at the picture when saying the sentence. Say *This is your family.* Group 1 repeats it, then group 2, and so on. Say *Ouch!* and let each group exclaim too.

● (L1) Ask if two children would like to come out and act the whole story.

**PB page 48
Ex. 1**
● (L1) Explain to the class that they have to look at the pictures, read both sentences and decide which one is right. They have to put a tick in the box opposite the correct sentence. Follow this procedure. (L1) Tell the class to look at the picture next to the first pair of sentences and they say what they can see. Then you read aloud the two sentences, and the children read them after you. Now they say which sentence is correct and put a tick in the right box. Go around and check their work.

**PB page 48
Ex. 2**
● Otto is eating lots of ice creams but is giving Drago one. (L1) Ask the class if they remember what happens when Drago tries to eat ice cream. (It melts!) Say *This is your ice cream* and write it on the board. Say the words as you write them and let the children look and say them. Trace the words in the air, with your back to the class. Say the words as you do so. Let the children, using their forefingers, copy you.

● They then trace over the words on their page with their fingers. Next they can join the dots together and finally write the sentence freehand. Go around and let each child read you the sentence. Help those children who find difficulty in forming letters and reading the sentence. They can colour in the picture.

Rhyme
- If there is time let the class listen to the rhyme that they will learn next lesson.

LESSON 3

New language	Known language
a drum	a star
black	bread

Preparation
- Draw a drum, a star, and a loaf of bread on the board and bring in a black card. Label each picture on the board. Have ready the flashcard 'black'.

PB page 49 Ex. 3
- Quickly write 1, —, 3, 4 on the board. Point to each numeral and give the children the opportunity to say 'one, —, three, four'. (L1) Ask them what comes between 1 and 3. Let a volunteer come out and write the number 2. (L1) Explain that in this exercise the children must fill in the missing letter or number. This means that they must remember which order the letters and numbers come in. Go around and check their work. Help those with difficulties. When they have finished write up the exercise on the board and go over it with the whole class.

Activity
- Point to each picture/word on the board and let the class say what it is. Hold up the black card and the flashcard 'black' and they say *black*. Write the word on the board. (L1) Tell them that you are going to play a game using these words. They have to know how to spell them. First point to each word and let the children spell them. For example say *black*. The children repeat it and they say 'b' 'l' 'a' 'c' 'k', the letter names. When you have done this with each word give them time to look at the words and remember them.

- Next divide the class into two teams. Ask the first player to spell a word, e.g. drum. Write the letters on the board as they are called out. If the player spells the word correctly, give a point to that team. If the player makes a mistake, offer the word to the first player in the other team. Give one point to the team that finishes the word correctly. The first team to get five points is the winner.

PB page 49 Ex. 4
- (L1) Explain to the class that they have to look at the pictures and decide what they are. Then they have to look at the letters underneath and find the other letters that match. Go over the first one, 'drum', with the class.

Rhyme
- Play the rhyme through to the class and join in the words. Play it again and encourage the children to join in. Play it a third time and everyone joins in.

This is my hand and this is my head.	This is your bike and this is your boat.
This is my cake and my bread.	This is your cat and your goat.
This is my egg.	This is your mouse.
This is my leg.	This is your house.
This is my book and my bed.	And this is your hat and your coat.

LESSON 1

New language	Known language	
	I like . . .	blue
	red	green
	yellow	

Preparation
- Bring in the red, yellow, blue and green coloured cards and their flashcards, also flashcards for 'I like red', 'I like yellow'.

Revision
- Play 'Cops and Robbers'. Take the children outside for this game or use an open area in the classroom. Divide the children into two groups, Cops and Robbers. Stand the groups behind lines facing each other. Put the four coloured cards on the ground about a third of the way from the Robbers to the Cops. Now point to each card and say its colour. (L1) Explain to the class that when you shout out a colour, the Robbers run and try to pick up the card and take it back across their line. If the Cops touch them before they cross their line they have to return the card.

Presentation
- (L1) Tell the class that you have a favourite colour, red. Show them the red card and say *I like red*. (L1) Check that they understand. Point to various red objects in the classroom, clothes, curtains, books, etc., and smile and say *I like red*. (L1) Ask if anyone else likes red. The children that do can say *I like red*. (L1) Ask who likes yellow. Those that like yellow can repeat after you *I like yellow*. Do this with a few colours. (L1) Check that they understand.

PB page 50
- Otto and Belinda are helping Pam to paint her boat. She is telling them that she likes red. When Pam goes away Belinda begins painting it yellow. What will Pam say? (L1) Check that the children understand and ask what Pam is saying and what Belinda is saying. (L1) Tell the children to look at the top picture and pretend to be Pam. Say *I like red*. (L1) Check that they understand. Let them repeat it after you. Do this a few times. (L1) Tell them to look at the bottom picture and pretend to be Belinda. Say *I like yellow*. (L1) Check that they understand. Say it again and let the class repeat it after you several times.

Practice
- Divide the class up into two groups, A and B. Tell group A they are Pam and group B they are Belinda. (L1) Remind them to look at the pictures when they say the sentences. Say *I like red*. Group A repeats it after you. Say *I like yellow* and group B says it. Change the groups around so group A is Belinda and group B is Pam. Let them say the sentences.

- Now divide the class up into their usual groups. Pretend to be Pam and say *I like red*. Each group repeats it after you in turn. Pretend to be Belinda and say *I like yellow*. Again each group repeats it after you.

- (L1) Ask if three children would like to come out and act the story.

Activities
- In this game players go through the alphabet, thinking of nouns that begin with the letters of the alphabet, e.g. Apples, Books, Cats, etc. Divide the class into two teams.

(L1) Tell the first player to think of something beginning with A, and to say *I like (apples)*. (L1) Tell the second player, (from the second team), to think of something beginning with B and say *I like (books)*. Alternate through the alphabet. Give players a few seconds to think of a word and let them consult their teams. Give one point for each sentence. The team with the most points at the end of the alphabet is the winner.

- If there is time the children can draw things that they like in their books. Go around and encourage them to say to you *I like . . . .* You can write the sentence that they give you in their exercise books.

LESSON 2

New language	Known language
	I like . . .
	blue

Revision

- Take the children out into the playground or use an open area in the classroom. Choose a child to be 'it'. (L1) Tell the others to run around while 'it' stands still. Then 'it' calls out a colour, e.g. *Blue!* He or she then chases anybody who is *not* wearing anything of that colour. When someone is caught, 'it' shouts *Out!* That child is out of the game. The children who are 'in' continue running around until 'it' shouts another colour and are chased again. You may like to change the child who is 'it' frequently. Play this for five minutes only.

Presentation

- Go around the class touching blue objects. Say *I like blue* several times. (L1) Check that the children understand and ask who likes blue. Those children repeat after you *I like blue*. They repeat it a few times. Touch green coloured objects and (L1) ask who likes green. Those that do say after you *I like green*.

PB page 51

- Otto is painting the boat too, but blue! Pam returns to find a multi-coloured boat, yellow, blue and red! (L1) Check that the children understand the situation and ask what colours can they see. How is Pam feeling? (L1) Tell them to look at the top picture and pretend to be Otto. Say *I like blue* a few times. Let the class repeat it after you.

Practice

- Divide up the class into their usual groups. Everyone pretends to be Otto. Say *I like blue* and group 1 repeats it after you, group 2, and so on.

- (L1) Ask if four children would like to come out and act the whole story. You could give them the coloured cards for the paint.

PB page 52 Ex. 1

- (L1) Explain to the class that they have to look at the pictures on the left hand and read the sentences on the right. One sentence only is right for each picture. They choose the correct one and put a tick in the box opposite the right one. Go through the task with the children. (L1) Tell them to look at the picture. Then you read the two sentences. They read each one after you. (L1) Ask which is right. They put a tick in the box. Go around and make sure that they are doing the exercise correctly.

PB page 52
Ex. 2

- Otto is a pirate on board a galleon. (L1) Ask the children who and what they can see. (L1) Explain that they have to colour in the picture carefully, using the right colours. Show them the key underneath so that they colour the 'bl' area in blue, etc. Go through the key and each colour with the whole class. Let them colour it in while you praise them. As you go around ask individual children to tell you what each colour is.

Song

- If there is time play the children the song they will learn in the next lesson.

LESSON 3

New language	Known language	
I like . . .	*parts of the body*	
colours	*animals*	
numbers		

Preparation

- Write 5, 6, 9 on the board and label them 'five', 'six', 'nine'.

- Draw coloured boxes, blue, red, green and yellow on the board and label them.

Revision

- Point to the numerals on the board and give the children the opportunity to say what they are. Rub out the numerals and point to each word and let the class say *five, six, nine*.

PB page 53
Ex. 3

- (L1) Explain to the children that in this exercise they have to read the lines of words and in each line there is an odd word, one which doesn't fit. Do the first example with the class. Read it and let the children read it after you. (L1) Ask which word is odd. Then do the same for numbers 2, 3 and 4. Go around and help those who have difficulties. Let individual children read the words to you.

PB page 53
Ex. 4

- Point to each coloured box on the board and let the class tell you their colours. (L1) Explain to the children that here they can choose their favourite colour and colour in the square. Then underneath they can write in the colour word and copy the sentence. Go around and help individuals.

Song

- Play the entire song through for the children to listen to while you join in the words. Play it a second time and encourage the children to join in the words. Play it a third time and all sing together.

> I like red,
> I like white,
> I like yellow and blue.
> I like green,
> I like brown,
> I like me and you.

Way in B: **Unit 14**

New language	Known language
bees	one–ten

Preparation
● Write numbers 1–10 on the board and label them 'one', etc.

Revision
● Quickly sing 'Ten Little Indians' from *Way in A* Unit 13, Lesson 3.

PB page 54
● Drago is looking for honey and Belinda is helping. Unfortunately the bees are returning to their home. They begin to chase Drago. (L1) Check that the children understand and ask who and what can they see. How does Drago feel? They can count the bees in the two pictures. Let them look at the top picture. (L1) Explain that the insects are bees. Say *bees* a few times and they repeat it. Count the bees aloud, *one*, *two*, *three*, etc. Let the children count them after you. Say *Eight bees*. They say *Eight bees* a few times. Count the bees in the bottom picture. The children count after you. Say *Nine bees* and they repeat it a few times.

Practice
● Divide the class into their groups. (L1) Remind them to look at the pictures as they count. Count from one to eight and let group 1 count after you, then group 2, etc. Say *Eight bees*, and each group repeats it after you. (L1) Tell them to look at the bottom picture. Count from one to nine. Each group counts in turn. Say *Nine bees*. Let group 4 repeat it after you, group 3, etc.

● (L1) Ask if any children would like to come out and act the story. Nine children can be bees (eight first and one can join in) and two children can be Drago and Belinda.

Activity
● Divide the class into two teams. (L1) Explain to them that you are going to call out a number and a child from each team has to run out and point to the correct numeral on the board. The first one to touch it wins a point for his or her team. Give every child the opportunity to have a turn.

● Now rub out the numerals, leaving the words, and play it again.

LESSON 2

New language	Known language	
one–ten	hens
bees	birds
apples	zebras

Preparation
● Draw two apples, hens, zebras, birds on the board and label them 'apples', etc. Make flashcards for each word.

PB page 55
● Drago has found a pool and jumps in to avoid the bees. He doesn't want to be stung! Belinda comes to help and squirts water at them. (L1) Check that the class understands the situation. (L1) Ask if anyone can tell the class what happened at the beginning of the story. Do they think the two friends will go looking for honey ever

again?! (L1) Tell the children to look at the top picture. Count the bees aloud, and let the children count after you. Say *Ten bees*. They repeat it a few times.

Practice

- Divide the class up into their usual groups. (L1) Remind them to look at the picture. Count to ten. Let each group count after you. Say *Ten bees*. Group 1 says *Ten bees*, then group 2, etc.

- (L1) Ask if any of the class would like to come out and act the whole story from beginning to end. You need twelve children altogether.

**PB page 56
Ex. 1**

- Point to each picture on the board and say *apples*, etc. Let the children repeat them after you. Next, hold up each flashcard and say the word. The children repeat it after you. Ask for volunteers to come out and match the cards to the pictures/words. Then rub out the words under the pictures and ask for other volunteers to come and match the flashcards to the pictures. Remember to praise and encourage them.

- (L1) Explain to the class that they have to look in their books at the objects in the circles and count them. Then underneath there are four phrases. They must read them and match them to the correct picture by copying the sentences underneath. Do the first example with the class. Read the four phrases to the children first and let them read them after you. (L1) Then ask what's in the first picture. Say *apples*. They repeat this. (L1) Ask what is in each picture and say *birds, hens, zebras*. They repeat each word after you. Next altogether count the apples. Say *Ten apples*. They repeat this. (L1) Tell them to write the phrase underneath. Do the same with the other circles. Go around and check that the children are doing the task correctly. Remember to praise and encourage them.

Rhyme

- If there is time let the children listen to the rhyme that they will learn next lesson.

LESSON 3

New language	Known language	
	stars	boats
	bees	shells
	flags	elephants

Preparation

- Draw two stars, bees, flags, boats, shells and elephants on the board and label them.

Activity

- Point to the pictures on the board and say each word. Let the children repeat them after you. Divide the class into two teams, A and B. (L1) Explain that you will say a word and a child from each team must run up and point to the right picture/word. Name the two children first, before you say the word. The first player to touch the picture wins a point for his or her team. Say each word once. Now rub off the pictures and play the game again. Say each word once.

**PB page 57
Ex. 2**

- (L1) Explain to the children that they have to count the objects in the picture, read the words at the bottom of the page and write the number of objects in the box. First of all read the words aloud, *stars, bees, flags*, etc. Let the children look at the words and say them after you. (L1) Next tell them to count the number of stars in the sky. They count up to seven. (L1) Tell them to put the number 7 in the right box. Go around and check that they have filled it in correctly. Do the same with each item. Remember to praise them.

Song • Play the song through for the children to listen to. Join in the words and do the actions. Play it again and encourage the children to do the actions and join in the words. Play it a third time so that you all sing it together.

This is the hive.
Where are the bees?
Can you see them in the trees?

Make a 'beehive' by interlocking the fingers of both hands.

Look at them fly,
Out of the hive,
One and two and three, four, five.

Take the fingers of one hand out and flutter them around, like flying bees.

LESSON 1

New language	Known language
I can see . . .	a hand
a man	

Preparation
- Draw a man on the board, or bring in a picture of a man.
- Have ready a piece of paper for each child to make a telescope.
- Make two flashcards: 'I can see a hand' and 'I can see a man'.

Revision
- Play 'I can see something beginning with (f)'. (L1) Remind the children of the game played in *Way in A* Unit 15, Lesson 1. Instead of saying the letter sound, say the name of the letter. (L1) Begin by telling the class that you are thinking of something in the classroom and they have to guess what it is. They listen for the *name* of the letter. Say *I can see something beginning with (b)*. They guess book, bike, etc. The first child to guess the correct answer can choose a letter. You might have to say the sentence for them.

Presentation
- Gather the children around you and look out of the window and say to the class *I can see a tree* (if you can!). Choose an object you actually *can* see and one for which the children know the English. Repeat the sentence. Let the children repeat it after you several times. Find another object. Say *I can see a house*. Say it again and let the children repeat it a few times after you. (L1) Check that they understand. Point to the picture and say *a man*. Say it a few times. Let the children repeat it after you.

PB page 58
- Otto is looking through a telescope. He can see a hand, then a man. Pam wants to look. (L1) Check that the children understand the situation and ask who and what they can see. What are the two friends doing? (L1) Tell them to look at the top picture. Pretend to be Otto, and say *I can see a hand*. (L1) Ask what Otto can see and check that the class understand the sentence. Say again *I can see a hand*. Let the children repeat it a few times. (L1) Tell them to look at the bottom picture: it's a picture of what Otto can see in his telescope. Say *I can see a man*. (L1) Check that the children understand. Repeat the sentence and let the class say it several times after you.

Practice
- Divide the class into their usual groups. They are to pretend that they are Otto. (L1) Remind them to look at the pictures as they say the sentences. Say *I can see a hand* and group 1 repeats it after you, group 2, etc. Then say *I can see a man*. Group 2 repeats it, group 3, etc.
- (L1) Ask if three children would like to come out and act the situation. One is Otto, a second is Pam and a third the man.
- Quickly draw a hand on the board. Say *I can see a hand*. Write the sentence underneath and say the words as you write them. Let the children repeat them after you. Point to the picture of the man on the board and say *I can see a man*. Write the sentence underneath and say the words. The children look and repeat them.

(L1) Show them the flashcards and ask children to match the flashcards to the sentences on the board. Let several children come out and match the cards. Rub out the pictures on the board. (L1) Ask for volunteers to come out and match the sentences.

Activity
- Give out a piece of paper to each child. Show them how to roll it up to make a telescope. Let them roll it up. Put yours to your eye and say *I can see a (chair)*. (L1) Tell the children that you are going to divide them into two teams, A and B. A child from each team takes it in turns to look into his or her telescope and say *I can see a . . . .* If an object is named that can be seen then the team gains a point.

LESSON 2

New language	Known language
Goodbye	That's my . . .
	father
	Pam

PB page 59
- Pam has seen that the man is her father. He's waving. It's time for Pam to go home. All the animals come to wave goodbye. (L1) Check that the children understand the situation and ask who the man is, where is Pam going? (L1) Explain that in the top picture Pam is saying that that is her father. Pretend to be Pam, and say *That's my father*. Say it a few times. Let the children say it after you. (L1) Tell them to look at the bottom picture and explain that the friends are saying goodbye to Pam. Say *Goodbye Pam* a few times and wave. Let the children say *Goodbye Pam* several times and wave as well.

Practice
- Divide the class into two groups, A and B. (L1) Tell group A that they are Pam and group B that they are all the animals. Pretend to be Pam. Say *That's my father*. Group A say it after you. Then say *Goodbye Pam* and wave. Group B repeat it and wave.

- Divide the class into their usual smaller groups. (L1) Remind the children to look at the pictures as they say the sentences. Pretend to be Pam, say *That's my father*. Each group repeats it after you. Then pretend that you are one of the animals, and say *Goodbye Pam* and wave. The groups repeat it after you in turn.

- (L1) Ask if six children would like to come out and act the story from the beginning.

PB page 60 Ex. 1
- (L1) Explain to the children that they have to look at the picture, read the two sentences underneath, and tick the correct box, i.e. the one opposite the right picture. Do the first one with the class. Ask *What's this?* They answer *A bird*. Read out the two sentences, and let the children read them after you. Then they say which is correct. (L1) Tell them to tick the right box. Do the same with the other three pictures and pairs of sentences. Go around and ask individual children to read the sentences. If they are unable to, read the sentence to them and they can read it after you. Remember to praise and encourage them.

Song
- If there is time let the children listen to the song that they will hear next lesson.

LESSON 3

New language	Known language	
	one–ten	a flag
	a bee	a star
	a tree	a shell

Preparation
- Write the letters L to Z on the blackboard at random – at child's height.

Activity
- Adding up. Divide the class into two teams. (L1) Explain that you will give each child two numbers and they have to add them up. If they are right then their team gains a point. Play it quickly.

  1) 1+3   4) 5+4
  2) 7+1   5) 3+2
  3) 8+2   6) 4+6

PB page 61 Ex. 2
- (L1) Tell the children that here are some numbers they can add up. They must write in the answers. Go around and help individual children.

Activity
- (L1) Tell the children that you are going to point to each of the letters L–Z on the board and they must say its name. Now some volunteers can come up and join the letters in order: L–M, M–N, etc.

PB page 61 Ex. 3
- (L1) Explain to the class that they have to join up the letters in order. Go around and help individual children.

Song
- Play the song to the children and join in the words. Play it again and encourage them to join in. Play it a third time and all sing it together.

  A, B, C, D, E, F, G,
  Clap your hands now, one, two, three.
  H, I, J, K, L, M, N,
  Count your fingers, eight, nine, ten.
  O, P, Q, R, S, T, U,
  I like yellow, I like blue.
  V and W, X, Y, Z,
  Touch your toes and touch your head!

Further suggestions
- To revise the second half of the alphabet you could play 'Winner says M' from *Bonanza*, using Z instead of M.

126